"*Bed and Board* is necessary and offensive
in the best possible way."

— Sarah Condon
author of *Churchy:
The Real Life Adventures
of a Wife, Mom, and Priest*

"…sage wisdom, biting humor, uncomfortable truths…
never a page that must be forgiven for
pedantic, sawdusty prose."

— Chad Bird
author of *Night Driving
Notes from a Prodigal Soul*

BED

&

BOARD

PLAIN TALK
ABOUT MARRIAGE

by

ROBERT FARRAR CAPON

A MOCKINGBIRD
PUBLICATION

Cover art and design by Tom Martin.
Published 2018 by Mockingbird Ministries.

ISBN-13: 978-0-9989171-1-5
ISBN-10: 0-9989171-1-7

Mockingbird Ministries ("Mockingbird") is an independent not-for-
profit ministry seeking to connect, comment upon and explore the
Christian faith with and through contemporary culture. Mockingbird
disclaims any affiliation, sponsorship, or connection with any other
entity using the words "Mockingbird" and "Ministries" alone or in
combination.

A nostalgic look at the way we were. Remembering our marriages and child-rearing styles in the 1950s and 60s could be illuminating. Perhaps we may even find a few gems worth polishing that could light our way back to the dinner table and one another. We may even discover that we can build happier communities under our very own roofs. Robert lived this as he wrote about it.

Valerie Capon
Shelter Island, NY 2017

CONTENTS

FOREWORD

THE ANTI-MARRIAGE-MANUAL
MARRIAGE MANUAL

T HIS LITTLE BOOK was originally released to great
acclaim in 1965. It was the first best-seller ever
written by a young Episcopal priest named Robert Farrar
Capon, who would go on to write many other books, con-
tribute to *The New York Times* as a food columnist, and
become one of the most widely celebrated flag-bearers
of God's grace. Even with such a legacy in his wake, the
bright light first cast by *Bed and Board* has never faded; it
has withstood the test of time, providing, for more than
half a century, a much-needed word of relief in a world
heavy-laden with marital expectations.

Having attended a whopping thirteen weddings in the
last year-and-a-half, I can safely say that contemporary
nuptial celebrations are always, first and foremost, beautiful

events—flawlessly decorated, heartwarmingly performed—but more often than not, wrought with anxiety. Even in the early planning phases, in that apocalyptic flurry of guest-list making and wedding cake tasting, wide-eyed brides and grooms often lose sight of the wonderful simplicity in this age-old promise: to love and to cherish, to have and to hold, in sickness and in health, till death do them part. Of course, a similar anxiety blossoms in marriage itself, where we so easily project onto our spouses the high expectations of who we *think* they should be: the yin to our yang, our one-in-a-million, our Soulmate. In 2016, *The Atlantic Monthly* wondered, "Is American Culture Asking Too Much of Marriage?" They interviewed relationship therapist Esther Perel, who said:

> We want one relationship to give us all the needs that have to do with anchoring and rooting and a sense of belonging and continuity and stability and predictability...and we still want that same person to also provide us a sense of novelty.... I want the same person to be familiar and to be new, and to be comfortable and to be edgy, and to be predictable and surprising.

No pressure, right? In his remarkably insightful book *Modern Romance*, comedian Aziz Ansari takes note of a similar puzzle. He explains that his parents, whose marriage was arranged, now seem happier than other couples who have taken a greater responsibility in crafting and maintaining the narrative of their love story. This kind of pressure often leaves us worrying that we could have done better. At some point, we may find ourselves asking: Is our relationship as good as it *could* have been? Did we marry the wrong person?

Although the challenges of contemporary marriage may, at first glance, seem altogether new and different from those of the 1950s and 60s, *Bed and Board* shows that the similarities outnumber the differences. Whatever it is that ails us is not circumstantial and remains ever with us, though generations come and go; it springs from who we are, not what we do. To this end, Robert's book is a delightful commentary on *people*, the goofballs who willingly enter into this impossible institution with such confidence, such bravado, and such lovely photography. Capon sees people as they really are: usually zoning out during premarital counseling, usually unsure of why they do what they do. Though writing well before the genesis of social media, he implicitly understands that we are never, not even a little bit, like the flawless mannequins we post online, the princes and princesses strolling through enchanted forests at sunset. As the original marriage myth-buster, Robert writes (plainly) that "the only candidates for marriage are sinners." He unmasks, in this book as in all of his books, something similar to what philosopher Yann Dall'Aglio said in his 2012 TED talk, "Love: You're Doing It Wrong":

> We are all imposters, a bit like a man on the street who appears totally cool and

indifferent while he has actually anticipated and calculated so that all eyes are on him. I think becoming aware of this general imposture that concerns all of us would ease our love relationships. It is because I want to be loved from head to toe, justified in my every choice, that the seduction hysteria exists. And therefore, I want to seem perfect so that another can love me. I want them to be perfect so that I can be reassured of my value.

Robert is always steering towards this conclusion: that we are all only human and as such, we are all in need. He became widely recognized as one of the first Christian writers who could communicate this truth clearly but also creatively, humorously, and without judgment. He's poetic. You'll want to take your time with this book and revel in Robert's rollicking sentences; note his genius, not just as a theologian, but as a writer and an artist.

Out of all of Robert's books, the whole collection of which is down-to-earth, *Bed and Board* is one of his most practical. It looks directly at everyday life and will likely affect how you see your day-to-day self—your marriage, your family, your relationship to God. That said, if you're holding this book as a newlywed, or an oldlywed, looking for marital advice or three surefire ways to keep your marriage aflame, I regret to inform you that you are, in fact, holding the wrong book. *Bed and Board* sees marriage as something that can neither fix nor be fixed; it is rather a dance to be enjoyed with bewilderment, and amusement. In this book, Robert weighs everything—not sorting swiftly through the puzzles of life but relishing them, laughing at them.

Of course, such boldness in the face of gritty practicalities simply could not be achieved in this mortal coil without a dash of controversy. Which is to say that by now Capon devotees will have noticed an elephant on the page. "You can't hide an elephant," Robert writes later in this book. "Unfortunately, it's even harder to hide a theologian." In this case, that theologian is Robert himself. I'm referring to his divorce, which left certain readers feeling that the initial hutzpah of *Bed and Board* had been undermined. Which is ridiculous. The minute we conflate Robert's life with a moral standard is the minute we forget the song of grace which is sung so beautifully and faithfully throughout this very book. At the time of *Bed and Board*'s original publication, Robert did not know that a long, happy, and—as I hear it—electric re-marriage awaited him. It was with our friend Valerie that Robert spent his last three decades of life. She adores this book precisely because she adores his voice, which endures on its pages; without her, this edition would not exist.

We're bringing back *Bed and Board* because it is not your average "how-to" manual; were it that, it would have failed, as all how-to manuals eventually do. *Bed and Board*, on the other hand, is something else, something entirely unconventional, something that outlasts its author's personal history. It is what Robert himself called, in his 1995 preface to *The Romance of the Word*, an "anti-marriage-manual marriage manual." In that same preface, he reflected on the various ways this book may seem dated, writing:

> Some of [*Bed and Board*'s] ethical stric-
> tures…I have since tempered; and since it
> was written before public consciousness of
> sexism had been raised (certainly before
> mine had), its language and a few of its atti-
> tudes were masculine to a fault. Nevertheless,
> the theology of the book—and above all its
> good-humored gratitude for having been
> allowed to embark on the leaky love boat of
> marital life—still, I think, stands up well.

It does. In my view, it is its unfailing levity regarding everyday life that resurrects *Bed and Board* day after day, keeping it fresh, relevant, and completely true no matter the decade. Robert finds humor in the distance between who we'd like to be and who we actually are—and the greatest humor of all, the pure absurdity, of who we are in God's eyes, his eternal beloved.

So, for the Capon initiate, *Bed and Board* may be the perfect place to start. You may enjoy discovering Robert *with* Robert, neither of you knowing exactly what God will teach you or where he will take you, the two of you lost together at sea in your brightly colored dinghy, simply amazed by it all.

But a seasoned Capon reader will also appreciate this book, perhaps even more so, since it recalls the man you know, who is so utterly *himself*—the playful, delightful wordsmith—but just a bit younger. Which brings me to yet another rewarding aspect of this edition: it is a snapshot of who Robert Farrar Capon was, and of what the Church was like; but, most importantly, it speaks the message of grace that our forebears, Capon's first readers, were so obviously moved by. A dip into that past, this book is now something even beyond its initially experimental "manual": it is a layered, beautifully constructed artifact of endless wonder. Like Robert's interpretation of marriage itself, this book is a dance. It's fun. And it's the perfect antidote for contemporary marital anxieties, because Robert never takes himself too seriously.

As Valerie suggests in her opening remarks, by looking into the past, we may be taken to a place as yet unvisited, a place of deeper understanding about who God is and where God would have us go. The pages of *Bed and Board* are full of compelling reflections, including, among other things, a poetic ode to the kitchen table, a particularly relevant treatise on materialism, and a touching note to the author's children. And all of that is just for starters. I speak for all of us at Mockingbird when I say that we are grateful to put our stamp on such a seminal work in the modern Christian canon.

CJ Green
Mockingbird Staff Editor
Charlottesville, VA 2017

BED

&

BOARD

To my family

I

ABSURDITY

The author celebrates the Holy Estate of Matrimony, professes disillusionment with the usual advices about it, and gives an all but disqualifying list of his qualifications for discussing it.

ARRIAGE IS HONORABLE IN ALL, and the bed undefiled. It is a very great sacrament indeed, and for all its troubles, its stock shows not the least sign of going down. And the family. Who can praise it as he should? Children like arrows in the hand of a giant; happy is the man whose quiver is full, whose wife is like the fruitful vine upon the walls of his house, whose children are like the olive branches round about his table. With sons like young plants and daughters like polished corners, he beholds how good and joyful a thing it is for brethren to dwell together in unity.

But be honest. The precious oil on Aaron's beard doesn't often reach the skirts of our clothing. It is hard to make a home. It is hard for one man and one woman to live together under one roof for as long as God wills. It is hard to raise a family—hard to manage the intractable results of bed and board without doing irreparable damage to somebody. And since it is nearly impossible to write about it without becoming clinical, pompous or gloomy, most of the published accounts of the matter are either depressing or dishonest—gray truth or rosy lie, but nothing very lifelike. It is hard to identify one's self with most marriage literature. Among the stern realities of religion, amid the triumphs of togetherness and the successes of sexual engineering, poor common garden humanity goes dumbly like a little lost peasant among grand personages. The clumsiness of *his* bed and the gibbering idiocy of *his* board bear little resemblance to these gray eminences and disgustingly healthy specimens. And so he wanders off back to his house convinced, not that he is unique (which he is) but that he is different (which he is not), and that he has somehow missed the boat, or the party, or whatever it was (he can't quite recall now) that it was supposed to be all about. All he remembers is that it seemed like a good idea at the time.

That peasant—Adam or Eve or you or me—needs a marriage book. But the ones he usually gets spend most of their time trying to put him at ease in the presence of the *grands seigneurs*: "Religion teaches…," they say; "Psychology tells us…," "Medicine indicates…." "All these noble subjects are your friends—they are here to help you." But what these books don't understand is that the peasant in us is not about to make friends with such beings just because somebody tells him they're nice people. Deep down inside he has an inescapable feeling that somehow he is not their dish; that, while they may well be the friends of everyone else in the world, they are not about to invite *him* to their house party. He is not proud of being thus a misfit—if anything he is a little ashamed. But he is a misfit and he knows it. Perhaps someday a book will be written that will reconcile him and them. Perhaps the definitive volume is on its way now, flowing serenely from the pen of the still-undiscovered great white hope of religious letters. Perhaps. But this book is not it. This is just something for him to read while he waits.

Its purpose is only to entertain him a while—and possibly to make him feel a little less unsure. It wants to tell him that he isn't the only one whose absurd life makes him feel like the exception to the rules. It has only one conceit to sell, and that is, that if he will take hold of Absurdity with both hands, he will be wiser than all the books that try to resolve it. Because life is absurd. It is like the square root of -1: You can do a lot with it, but you can't do much about it. And everything that is central in life is absurd in proportion to the degree of its centrality. Saving one's money, not very; Stamp collecting, a little; Music, quite; Love and Marriage, tremendously; and Birth, Death and Faith, absolutely. Our peasant has his hand on a very large truth, and no slick reconciler should ever be allowed to talk him out of it.

Accordingly, this book is not about those giants who tower over him: Psychology, Education, Maturity, Sexual Adjustment—not even Religion. They can take care of themselves. This is about him—that is, about me (for we are all unique, and practically identical). This is, to be honest, not a book at all. It is only a monologue, and not an entirely sober one at that. It is one peasant swapping stories with another in the cold backyard of the House of Important Subjects, while the *grands seigneurs* hold their solemn consultations within. The author's qualifications therefore almost cease to matter. Indeed, he has arranged things so that only one is really necessary: He must be an expert in absurdity. And that is the only one that will be offered. An absurd Baedeker for an absurd journey; no apologies, no explanations.

Ideally, I suppose, the best method would be something more scholarly: select quotes from reliable authors, careful synthesis, and a string of definite conclusions. But out here in the courtyard around the fire that procedure is hardly realistic. The pressure of our paradoxes has a way of rendering us all impatient of neat lectures. So instead of doing it the right way and handing the reader neatly arranged snippets from the old masters, I am going to do it the wrong way and give him my own precooked, prechewed and predigested version of a few items. I propose to regale him with some random opinions on Husbandhood, Wifeliness, Bed and Board—with a few personal comments, not on the Important Subjects which haunt us, but on those vastly more important subjects: ourselves, our roles and our places. We were created not to draw intellectual arabesques about life, but to live; our roles matter more than our rules. We are the subjects, not they. The method is probably questionable, and it is certainly personal. But at least the reader won't get eyestrain.

To begin, then: I am a priest of the Episcopal Church. This is the first of my absurdities. Absurd in all seriousness, because the Incarnation of God, his Cross, his Resurrection, his high-priestly Intercession, his Church, his grace, and his choosing of men—of me—are all roaringly, marvelously absurd; all lavish, fantastic gifts, receivable only by lavish, fantastic givers. But it is my first paradox in a less serious sense, too, for to be an Episcopalian is to pile paradox upon itself. The Episcopal Church is the absurdest version of a supremely absurd religion. (I have been her son all my life—I am reveling in my mother's foibles, not being disrespectful.) Catholic and Protestant, authoritarian and individualistic; believing in bishops but not giving them power, believing in priests but not letting on; stylish in some places and dowdy in others, capable of real prophecy and of double-talk out of both sides of her mouth, she is indeed all things to all men, a measure stretched far out of shape, partly by carelessness but partly by her gallant attempt to encompass the boundless grace of God.

But beyond being a priest of the Episcopal Church, I have a further absurdity. I am married, and happily at that, though little of it is my doing. (Congratulatory telegrams should properly be sent to God, Mother Nature and the many others near and dear who have so kindly picked up after me.) For marriage is a paradox second only to life itself. That at the age of twenty or so, with little knowledge of each other and a dangerous overdose of self-confidence, two human beings should undertake to commit themselves for life—and that church and state should receive their vows with a straight face—all this is absurd indeed. And it is tolerable only if it is reveled in as such. A pox on all the neat little explanations as to why it is reasonable that two teenagers should be bound to each other until death. It is not reasonable. It happens to true life, but it remains absurd. Down with the books that moralize reasonably on the subject of why divorce is wrong. Divorce is not a wrong; it is a metaphysical impossibility. It is an attempt to do something *about* life rather than *with* it—to work out the square root of -1 rather than to use it.

Up with the absurdity of marriage then. Let the peasant rejoice. He is a very odd ball on a very odd pool table, and his marriage is one of the few things left to him that will roll properly in this game. And up with the marriage service. Let the peasant go back and read it while he rejoices—preferably in the old unbowdlerized version still used by the Church of England. It is full of death and cast iron. And it is one of the great remaining sanity markers. The world is going mad because it has too many reasonable little options, and not enough interest or nerve to choose anything for good. In such a world, the marriage service is not reasonable, but it is sane; which is quite another matter. The lunatic lives in a world of reason, and he goes mad with making sense; it is precisely paradox that keeps the rest of us sane. To be born, to love a woman, to cry at music, to catch a cold, to die—these are not excursions on the narrow road of logic; they are blind launchings on a trackless sea. They are not bargains, they are commitments, and for ordinary people, marriage is the very keel of their commitment, the largest piece of ballast in their small and storm-tossed boat. Its unqualified hurling of two people into their deathbed is absurd, but so is the rest of that welter of unqualified hurlings we call life. You cannot contract out of being born, out of crying, out of loving, out of dying; you cannot contract out of marriage. It may be uncomfortable, it certainly is absurd; but it is not abnormal.

My final qualifying absurdity is the full equal of my others. I have six children. The number is not the point, though for the record, they are two boys and four girls in the sequence BGBGGG. The point is that nothing is more absurd than begetting. Having fits is more reasonable than having children. First, because *they* are absurd— and impossible, and unmanageable besides. There are days—lots of days—when, if I could, I would mail them all back to Dr. Spock. Second, because it is absurd to give them houseroom. I manage badly enough keeping my own ship afloat. What am I doing cluttering this already crowded anchorage with more ships and more masters?

For that is the secret, you know. They are not members of my crew; they are the masters of their own vessels. Their presence with me is that of a not entirely peaceable boarding party; and they will leave when *they* please, not I. Down, then, with Gesell and Ilg. The peasant knows what we all suspect. It's them or us, and eventually it's going to be them. And we have the short end of the stick, for with all the power of our absurd hearts we love them, and are hopelessly caught.

And that will do for preliminary qualification. I have some other absurdities which will appear in due course. I will simply list them here. I live in a very large house. I teach dogmatic theology and Greek, keep a decent cellar, and know something about wines, cooking, music, praying and living (in approximately that order). We get too soon old and too late smart, but with a loving God and forgiving friends, I am grateful and glad. It is cold out here in the yard, but we have a few more sticks and lot more time, so poke the fire again, Billy; we'll sup before we go.

II

WEDDINGS

Select glimpses of premarital counseling—a desperate and intractable subject—together with a futile protest against the iron-fisted folkways that govern the ceremony.

BOUT THE BEGINNING OF MY OWN MARRIAGE I remember very little. There is seldom much to recall about the days on which we are born. (Of my ordination to the priesthood, for example, I retain only two things: choking up during the singing of "St. Patrick's Breastplate," and the stunning weight of the hands laid on me as I knelt in the dark circle of priests.) Nor should we expect to remember much of such occasions. They are obscure and decisive instants of transition—days on which we pass through the dead center of real motion. Intelligible activities precede and follow them, but they themselves remain absurd. All I can clearly recall of my wedding day is the heat, and my father-in-law's rented full-dress shirt collar wilting visibly as the minutes passed. It was 95 in the shade.

As a priest, of course, I have seen a fair number of weddings since, hot and cold. There has been, over the years, the usual procession of unusual couples: couples full of ideas, couples without a glimmer; bright and articulate ones, stony and silent ones; managerial brides, uninvolved grooms—all the marvelous assortment that our much-touted system of marriage arrangement by free choice and romantic love brings forth with a lavish hand. Some-times I wonder whether the system is all it's cracked up to be—whether we are any better off than we were in the days when Papa and Mama arranged the whole thing. On balance, it is very nearly a draw. Interestingly, it makes not the slightest difference to the Church. Her marriage rite was written in the days of arranged marriages, and hasn't changed much since. She is not nearly so concerned with why the bride and groom think they want to get married as with what they propose to do about it from here on out. She knows, peasant that she is, that with anything that big, their ideas about it will be only so many flies buzzing around the elephant. It is the feeding and water-ing of the leviathan of their commitment that the mar-riage rite is about.

What the wedding is about is another story. The Church wrote the words, and she is in dead earnest about the occasion, but I'll tell you something about the attendant ceremonies. Do you know where all the ritual directions come from—I mean the ones about choosing the pattern of the silver and the number of the brides-maids, the color of the gowns and the length of the veils? Do you know who decreed the little white prayer book lashed onto the small bouquet, or the hesitation step up the aisle? Do you know who spoke the fiat that set Lohengrin in his unswerving course, and seated the bride's mother for all eternity? Not the Church. She is one of us. I'll tell you who it was; it was somebody over in that house—Babylon the Great, most likely. One of her friends arranges all the funerals. And a very nice little concession it is, too, whereout they suck no small advan-tage.

But that's not the point. All I want to say is that I don't like weddings, and I do like the marriage rite, and that I feel very funny about doing what I have to do. We sit down, they and I, for a couple of sessions of what the canon law blithely refers to as "instructing the parties as to the nature of matrimony." But being in the same room is about as close as we ever get to each other. I talk *marriage*; they think *wedding*. I tell them that the average wedding is a kind of irrelevant fling with no connections before or after—a preoccupation with the details of thirty minutes at the expense of the commitments of a lifetime. They listen with glazed, enraptured eyes. I urge them to steep themselves in the words of the rite, to eat, drink and breathe its atmosphere. I expound it, line by glorious line. Then I invite them to dialogue - to pursue its richness together. Do you know what questions, what comments, they have? Do you know what they ask me? They want to know if they can have the rehearsal an hour earlier, because his cousin Frances who is one of the bridesmaids has a hairdresser's appointment at eight. (What do you do for a living, Billy? Do you know anybody who wants a good wine steward?)

That is about the way it goes. The wedding as a decisive instant of transition vanishes behind endless yards of tulle; their first appointment with their common destiny is missed in the shuffle of incidental arrangements. Mercifully however they forget it all, and learn it the hard way over the years. Still, I wish they could hear it, and year after year I keep polishing the instructions. I suppose they are good for me, if nothing else. Here is one, for instance.

A couple of years back there was a cartoon that showed two clams sitting at the bottom of the ocean. One of them says to the other, "But you wouldn't buy a new car without first driving it, would you?" My pre-marital couple doesn't crack a smile. Not an eye blinks. Nobody's punch lines fall flatter than a priest's in marriage instructions. As far as they are concerned, I am only supposed to be a "minister of religion." Like in the movies. The predictable vicar who thinks life is about afternoon teas and long walks. No matter, I press on. I raise the subject of premarital chastity as such. It is not old-fashioned, I tell them, or if it is, it has yet to go out of date as far as the facts are concerned. What do you think you have to practice for marriage? They watch me blankly, but they are watching. Well, you don't have to practice going to bed together. And you don't have to, because you can't. Premarital intercourse is not the same thing as the marriage bed. Of course there is something unique about the first time whenever it comes, but if it comes before, there is inevitably attached to it the fillip of the forbidden. It doesn't matter how enlightened people are, or how blasé the society is; our mores, honored in breach or observance, are our mores, and we're stuck with them. We might as well try to change our air. Do it now, I tell them and doing it later will have the edge taken off it to say the least. People think of the flesh as a mighty monster straining at the leash, bursting with health and unquenchable vigor. What they don't know is that poor flesh takes an awful drubbing. It's not *all* in the head, but a good bit of it is. Brother Ass is pretty easily confused, and there are a lot of wedding nights that are not nearly as funny as the jokes about them.

So forget about practicing *that*, I tell them. You'll have plenty of time later. Try to make the start as much of a start as you can. Licit sex usually runs a poor second to illicit; don't make any more comparisons than you can help. What you really need to practice is keeping promises. Right now of course you wouldn't go to bed with anybody else, but later on, it's not always that clear, and then these little exercises in fidelity will be worth something in terms of chastity and trust. So, I say, if you have so far been chaste, don't let anyone talk you out of it. And if you haven't been, well, try and cut out the compromises. Even a tardy dose of principle is better than none.

Well, that usually produces something of a studied silence. I don't try to be embarrassing, but since there is in fact a lot of premarital gun-jumping even among professing Christians, and since it is usually justified with fairly highfaluting reasons, I feel obliged to say it. Fancy reasons or not, it makes an already tricky job even harder. But I also feel obliged to suggest that they do something utterly outlandish besides. I tell them not only to be chaste but to be modest—to cut out not only the intercourse, but all the little semi-moral approximations to it: the petting that everybody takes for granted. Because that doesn't help much either. If it involves any worthwhile and pleasurable discoveries, it would be much more comforting to make them later amid a pile of unpaid bills where they could lighten the load of lifelong monogamy. It is really too bad to fumble one's way through them greedily in the back seat of some car when they could be savored and relished at leisure on a long winter evening. And if it doesn't involve worthwhile discoveries—if it is only that preoccupied and perverse scratching of itch by fetish which so often passes for sexuality among us—then it is best simply to skip it before marriage, and afterward, too.

And at that point, I am sure I lose them every time. Chastity before marriage is pretty far out, but modesty is a real joke, like virginity in the late Roman Empire. I have never had the nerve even to wonder whether any of it gets across.

Anyway, that gives you an idea. I have some other comments, but they can wait till later. Right now while the water boils for tea, I shall give you, rapid-fire, a couple of bits and pieces. I am in favor of formal public engagements with full family approval. (This is partly special pleading; with two sons, four daughters, and no counties heard from as yet, I am trying to hedge my bets.) I think people should finish school before marriage and acquire some direction in life. And I am all for retreats before weddings, nuptial masses, the replacement of Mendelssohn by Purcell, receptions with decent menus, and starting out without contraception. I am against double ring ceremonies, twin beds, Schubert's "Ave Maria," short bridal gowns, cheap champagne, looped bridegrooms, most receptions, and weddings held in church for no Christian reason. The world, as you might suspect, shows no signs of beating a path to my door for premarital advice, and I may well have a lot of it wrong, but if I can persuade even one couple to sass the system back, I think I may have a function.

III

IMAGES

An inquiry into the matrimonial pictures in our heads; praise for a few of them, alarm at most of them, and a shot in the dark at finding some better ones.

BUT ENOUGH OF THIS PREMARITAL MADNESS. None of it cuts any mustard at all. The fuse of the population explosion gets set anyway, the caps are wired, and the magneto is pushed with gay abandon. We have had nearly twenty years now of more or less headlong attempts at family life, and it seems that the end is not yet. Not that marriage as such is in very great shape—with the divorce rate on the way up, that flattering unction can be put back in the jar—but that people's goals for their marriages did make a little more sense in the 1950's than they did in the Roaring Twenties or the

Gasping Thirties. I don't know why, for example, we all started having children as if they were going out of style. I would like to think that I did it for Christian reasons, but I don't think they account for too much; I think the number of children people have has very little to do with the price of any eggs, sacred or secular. At different times Christians have, in all sincerity, made a point of having one or two—or ten or twelve. So it isn't Christianity that made the difference—nor even the failure to know what Christianity was about. And the secularists are no better. Some of them claim that it's economics that governs the birth rate. But as often as not, it's the people who can afford the fewest who have the most. What really makes it tick is more mysterious than all the likely, half-valid explanations. And since I don't know much about everybody, I'll tell you why I think *I* had a large family. (Why I *think*, mind you, not why I know; because even now I'm not sure.)

First of all, I always intended to have a big family, if possible. That much was a kind of axiom. But where the idea came from is harder to say. Partly I suppose from having been an only child, but that's not enough. Quite apart from the idea of more company, a big family represented to me something solid, something deeply rooted in the past. And it was the idea of having roots in the past that really sold me. I became an old fogey young; I looked backward habitually and gladly. So, I think, did a good many of my generation. The real question therefore is: Where did this love of the past come from?

Well, I think it came from living just one age after the end of the modern era. I grew up reading *Popular Science Monthly* in the thirties. I will never forget its rapt narration of the coming wonders of the new age; but I don't think we will ever see that dewy-eyed scientific Messianism again. Back there, in the dark of the depression, newness was still the great watchword, just as it had been in the twenties. At Hiroshima, the newness blew itself sky-high, and when we finally did crawl out of our holes, we all began to look around for something a little less violently new. *The Waste Land* was no longer an avant-garde way of talking about life; it was the way our world *felt*. We emerged from the storm by the skin of our teeth, with a new appreciation of the need for better boats and better masters, and we looked to the past to teach us how to build them. I don't say we all *thought* about it that way, but I do think that is what most of us did. Because the love of the past wasn't just a private quirk with me; it was the hallmark of the fifties: colonial furniture, Early American prints, big kitchens and open fireplaces; the restoration of dining rooms, pewter and milk glass, the heyday of folk music, togetherness, Admiral Rickover and reading with phonics. It was a mixed bag, and it had its share of monsters, but matrimonially speaking, it hung together pretty well. Somewhere after the start of the Cold War, we all began to gather around the hearth to learn to bake our own bread again. We were not modern. Our parents who were young in the twenties were the ones who were modern. We were old-fashioned. And so were all the Michaels and Abigails, the Honors and the Deborahs, the plain Jonathans and the even Stephens we begot. How long it will last I don't know; but those numerous offspring have smelled something they will never forget. Of course, along with it all we have drowned them in commercial bilge, stuffed them with TV dinners and surrounded them with the racket of four appliances running at once; we have bequeathed them insoluble problems, and precious little discipline with which to handle them. But if, on some distant day, the smell of fresh bread can still break their hearts, I do not think that all will have been too hopelessly lost.

In other words, while I can take just as much professional glee as the next priest in clucking my disapproval at the dreadful encroachments of secularism, I cannot say I am sorry to have served my marital apprenticeship in the fifties. It was not a bad age as ages go. We built something with our own hands. We may yet knock it down again, but Spoon River style, we did it ourselves, and we built it as high as the White House. Do you know why we joked about Jack and Jackie? Because we had won—we could afford to smile. They were us, up there on top, with our own family football and our own slightly overdone longhair pretensions. And do you know why we cried at his funeral? We cried because our own flower had been cut—and because it was the supreme moment of a generation in love with old-fashioned rightness. She dug that funeral out of the roots of the past; and she made it live. Lucinda Matlock walking down Pennsylvania Avenue, in the waning sunlight of the nuclear age. I can throw brick-bats with the best of them, but I can brag too, and I will not be ungrateful. In a century given to the overproduction of very small wines, that was a magnificent vintage and, by George, we managed it.

Well, anyway, we managed the front end of it. We have yet to bring off the rest. And one vision, one vicarious triumph, won't do it, though it helped mightily. We have had some bright ideas, but what we need now are detailed directions. My wife can stand there reaching me warm bread for only a small part of any given day. I can preside impressively as *paterfamilias* at my Vermont rock maple dining table only seven short and distracted times a week. What do we do the rest of the time?

I would like to think that all I need to do to answer that one is to go to Mother Church. I would like to hope that, stored in the treasuries of her wisdom, she has the minute and careful instructions I want. But I'm afraid she does not, at least not in any shape that is about to make them presently and easily available. I do think that one way or the other they are there. But I suspect that nobody can put his hand on them; that they have been misfiled, or left in old boxes to which nobody has keys; and that the few instructions there are, are written in ancient tongues for which there are no translators.

Of course, she does tell me that the root out of which it all grows is commitment to marriage as a vocation, as the call of God to me. I have preached sermons like that myself. I have told the faithful that they must nail themselves to their callings—that they will be saved by their obedience to the work God gives them to do. I have urged them to go out from the altar rail and be Christian fathers and mothers, and Christian husbands and wives, and brothers, sisters, sons and daughters. But at that point I begin to get blank looks. And the trouble isn't with the word Christian. They know pretty well what that means. They have been taught, and they have even taken some of it in. It isn't the spiritualities that confuse them. When I tell them to pray, for example, they have some idea of what I mean even if they don't do much of it. And ditto for things like receiving the sacraments, and repenting, and believing. But they can't run right out and be Christian fathers and mothers, because they have next to nothing in their heads about what being a plain father or mother looks like in this day and age. It does no good to preach up a storm about the salutary results of sticking to one's last, when they don't know what a last is and have probably never seen even a single shoe made on one. As a matter of fact, such preaching is dangerous. It leaves the distinct impression that on the level of practice the Church is full of baloney. And to be honest, it is. It's not only in marriage that Christians are urged to the accomplishment of glorious goals without being given a shred of practical help. They get lectures about sacrificial giving, for example, but all too often they get no description of what and how much it means in terms of cold cash. Or they hear glowing exhortations about commitment among the faithful, but they are subsequently sent out to sell cookies and baked beans in front of the A & P so that the fuel bills they haven't put up enough money to cover can be paid for with the small change of the unconverted.

So when the Church tells them to be Christian parents, it should have something pretty snappy up its sleeve on the subject of parenthood, if they are not to go away despondent or scornful. And that is exactly where the whole thing falls flat. Take fatherhood, for example. The Church has some pictures of Victorian fatherhood or colonial fatherhood, but what about fatherhood now? They can find lovely old tintypes of Father as the head of the household directing the evening's conversational exchanges in a setting of silence and decorum, but what has that got to do with their dinner tables where for years everybody has been talking at once while the TV flickers and the telephone rings? They can be shown the old engraving of Father as the priest and teacher of his family, dispensing the word of God and the multiplication tables over the open Bible, but what does that mean to them? All the teaching anybody is about to stand for is done in school; and as for his priestly functions, Father wouldn't recognize them if he fell over them. Religion belongs first to the clergy, next to the children and then to their mother. It is only *in articulo mortis* that it gets even within hailing distance of Pop.

Therefore the march forward cannot be conducted to the beat of an antique drum. If there are going to be Christian spouses or Christian families, they will have to start from scratch; the old patterns just can't be transferred.

Charming though they might be, they don't fit any more, and those who try them on succeed only in looking silly. But if the old hats are out of style, what is there instead? To tell the truth, not much. The Christian mind has lo, these many years been pretty well switched off as far as ordinary life is concerned. It has taken what was available without asking any questions. Of course, in religion and morals it tried to do its own cooking; but across the rest of life—schooling, housing, marrying; working, playing, spending—it has been content to buy whatever packaged mixes were available on the shelves of the secular idea market.

The result is that Christians, who would like to think they were different, have only succeeded in making themselves indistinguishable. They, who would like to hope they had the answers, have only the same questions as the rest of the world. And so they sit on the sidelines, capable of an occasional pious comment, but utterly unable to tell themselves or anyone else how to go about doing the ordinary jobs that constitute nine-tenths of the raw material of their salvation. Where does it go from here? The antique drum stirs no souls, the old tintypes are merely funny, and the current pictures are not yet developed. Who is going to come up with the saving, imaginative solution?

Much as it may surprise you, the answer is, *we* are. You and I, the heirs, assigns, and devisees of the 1950's, are going to revive the Christian mind. We, who strummed our guitars in the plush trenches of the Cold War—we, the triumphant restorers of the dining room table, the inveterate adders of extra bedrooms—we are going to try to begin to start to think again. Of course maybe there aren't enough of us and maybe we won't make it; but what's the sense of talking like that? Absurdity is the touchstone of our calling. We've got one leg on the deciding rubber, and the best-looking cards the modern world has dealt all this long evening; if we don't try for at least a small slam, we'll never forgive ourselves.

But first of all we shall have to be very clear about the nature of what we're looking for—about what is really involved in an imaginative solution. We like to think, of course, that we think; but what people allow to pass for thinking is usually about 90 percent reshuffling of images. They form their lives, spend their money, and choose their wallpaper on the basis of pictures in their heads. And a whole industry devotes itself effectively to the production and maintenance of the necessary images. Madison Avenue sleeps not day or night and it shows a tidy profit for its zeal. Thinking by pictures of course can be dangerous—any system that involves responding to stimuli rather than taking the initiative makes us liable to being led around by the nose. But we do in fact think that way, and understanding it explains a good deal about our poverty of thought on the subject of family life. For example, when it first occurs to my conscious mind that it might be a good idea to try a pack of Salem cigarettes, it isn't because I reasoned my way discursively to that conclusion. The battle for my patronage was fought and won in the unconscious, where somebody was busy showing me pictures of pretty girls, clean-cut young men, springtime scenery—and Salem. And the precise reason why it does not occur to my conscious mind to run out and buy a particular brand of fatherhood is that nobody has been showing me pictures of that at all. At least not ones I can identify with.

Unrealistic ones, of course, I see all the time: the old chromos; the little commercial sketches of Daddy tucking the kiddies in bed while the absolute matriarch stands by deciding what appliance he will buy next; the ridiculous cartoons of Pop as the lovable village idiot, outwitted at every turn by even the smallest of his children. (It's fascinating to realize that, dreadful though they are, these pictures are not so much lies as maudlin half-truths. They are actually detached bits of really good pictures—random details of old Christian masterpieces thrown together in a secular pastiche.) My imagination is being fed, but on that diet it gets precious little nourishment. Unfortunately, however, the malnutrition of the imagination cannot be cured by the imagination itself. It cannot feed upon what it has not seen, and it cannot see what it has not been fed; it is stymied by its own nature. The imaginative solution therefore is a misnomer. It is precisely the solution that does not start with the imagination at all, but with two less exciting but more durable quantities: with an abstract knowledge of principles, and an honest recognition of facts.

A little over a century ago, some priests of the Church

of England, sitting in dusty libraries in Oxford, made a discovery. The Church of England, they found, was actually catholic in the old sense of the word, and not, as everybody seemed to assume, protestant in the modern sense. The idea struck like lightning and started a rather large number of fires. It meant, for example, that the correct mode of worship for Anglicans every Sunday morning was not the service of Morning Prayer which everyone was used to, but the Holy Communion which people saw only about four times a year. The Anglo-Catholics said this out loud. Full of confidence in the persuasive power of abstract rightness, they spelled out the principle in tracts of monumental length. Unfortunately, nobody was convinced. And they were unconvinced because when they went to their imaginations to find something about the order of Christian worship, they found only an album full of pictures of Matins at eleven. So they turned to the Anglo-Catholics and told them: no sale. With varying degrees of politeness, but with uniform firmness, they advised them to get their hands off the ecclesiastical applecart, and suggested that they go fly their Roman kite where it would be appreciated.

Some of them did. But among the many who didn't, there were a few geniuses. They reflected. If people won't go to Communion every Sunday because they can't imagine themselves going to Communion every Sunday, because they have never seen people going to Communion every Sunday, why not show them some pictures of people doing just that? And here is where the genius came in. They looked at their abstract principles: Communion every Sunday was the only possible conclusion. And then they took a good honest look at the facts; the only conclusion there was that nobody was going to talk the Church out of Matins at eleven. And out of these unreconcilable truths, in the darkness of an unstocked imagination, they came up with the brilliant solution: *Start another service at eight!* Make it Communion. Get anyone you can to come to it. And keep it up for years.

It was simple—absurdly simple. But it worked. Pictures began to be drawn. At first people found them funny. By and by, they took them for granted. Eventually they found them plausible. And finally they began to conclude that the thing wasn't a bad idea after all. We are still living in the backwash of that stroke of genius—of that imaginative solution which was made with no images at all, but which grew up to provide them for generations to come. The eight o'clock service is as normal now as Matins at eleven once was. No one can imagine the Church without it. And it hasn't stopped at eight. The not-so-old old system is on the way out. History is passing it by. In its place is arising the very ancient new way with its early Communions at eight and its family Eucharists at nine-thirty, with its late Celebrations at twelve-forty-five and its evening Masses at six. And all because somebody had the brilliance to take hot principle and cold fact, and, by unimaginable ingenuity, bring forth a new image.

The point of this long excursion should by now be fairly clear: As far as family life is concerned, we are in exactly the same kind of boat. We have some principles to rediscover, and some images to build. And we are going to have to do it about the same way: by sitting down, cold-turkey, in front of the books till we have found the root truths, and in front of the facts till we stop kidding ourselves about how well it's going. And then, very carefully and very boldly, we must put one and one together. It will not get done by waiting till we have pictures of what it should look like. Nobody, right now, can imagine the right solution.

Did you hear that? Did you hear the blessed word? It was *Nobody*. Not Gesell, not Ilg, not Spock, not the Ford Foundation; not Paul VI, not Walter Lippmann, not Madison Avenue and not the Institute for Advanced Studies. It was *Nobody*. They have called *our* name, Billy. We have won the drawing. The world is waiting for the brilliant nonentities who are about to invent the eight o'clock service of fatherhood, or the nine-thirty Eucharist of true wifeliness. It is waiting for us, standing out here in the wings, to pick the thing up in the dark, and, on the basis only of what we *know*, to work it out our own way. Sure we're scared—and doubtful too—but so was the fellow who first unlocked a Victorian church three hours early. And sure we don't know what we're doing, and sure we feel funny and self-conscious and tempted to skip it. But so did he, and he made it. And we will too, provided we are willing to be bold and a little foolish. Imaginative solutions are never imaginable beforehand; dusty truth plus honest fact equals fresh start.

IV

ROLES

The shot in the dark pursued; dead canards brushed aside, and a shaky light pointed at some of the stones thus uncovered. Human nature, Husbandhood and Wifeliness displayed; praise for Patriarchs and Fat Mothers.

THE JOB, THEN, IS TO BEGIN dusting and being honest; and since we are inclined to be a little more discerning about our facts than our principles, we can spend less time on that factor of the equation. There's no need to labor them; everybody and his brother takes a crack at criticizing the difficulties of modern life. The fact is that the facts are not good. We live in an age that, for all its multiplication of red-hot aids to living, is characterized increasingly by a singular lack of concern about *how* to live. Excellence has a hard time meeting competition in any age, but in ours we have made a real specialty of shoddiness and shallowness. We float with the tide. Our idea of the right direction is keeping our backs to the wind. Worse yet, our ability to mass-produce our specialties has surrounded us with more distractions than any age has ever had. There is more to hear, more to read, more to watch, and more to taste than even kings ever dreamed. We have arranged matters so that a man can go from kindergarten to the old-age home so surrounded by things to do that he need never decide what he *is*. The one question he must not ask is: Who am I? If he should happen to wonder, somebody quickly gets him a lollipop, or a new car, or another wife or a stronger tranquilizer. And the worst part of it is that the somebody, more often than not, is himself. If we were only the victims of distraction it would be bad enough, but we are its agents too. We want these things. Be honest. I choose the junk on TV more often than I do Channel 13. So do my children. So do you. The world is slowly drowning in an ocean of garbage and all we do is measure each day's new high-water mark.

It is highly unlikely therefore that we will make very good marriages. And we don't. Even with the best intentions, the odds are so against our ever discovering what we are really for that the ship of matrimonial bliss seldom gets anything more than a canned launching ceremony. We fasten no chains to it, send no tugs after it, have no dock at which to moor it, no machinery with which to fit it, not enough money to finish it, and not enough knowledge to sail it if we did. But we keep right on with the launchings. And after the champagne pops and the guests wander off, the ships do too: wonderful ideas floating aimlessly down the drab tidal rivers to their final rusty rest on the flats.

So now I have had my crack at criticizing too. It's fun, and it's easy. Too easy. Not that it isn't worth something to know that the trash is already up to the windowsills on the second story, but that it's not enough to let it go at that. It's time to get on to the real question: What is it that we're supposed to be? Where are the principles on which some kind of new approach to marriage can be based? It will be hard enough to put them into operation when we find them; with the facts so against us, we should at least be in a hurry to start looking.

You can't hide an elephant. There will be very few surprises in this book. The root principles, the dusty master keys, are where they always were—in history, and in the principal documents: the Bible and the marriage rite. We don't have to invent them. But it will help to be able to recognize them when we trip over them—a familiarity which can be acquired only by extensive travel with open eyes. We shall have to go back and dig around in documents and sources until recognition is forced upon us by the repeated barking of our shins on the old intractable ideas. We must not think of it as a lark, a brief exegetical expedition in search of the obvious. What we are looking for is indeed obvious, but not to us; and that makes for a hard cruel journey. If we don't know what to look for, we can hardly expect to know when we've found it. As a matter of fact, we don't even know where to begin. The elephants live where they like. Their habitations are obvious to well-trained elephant hunters, but not to the likes of us, whose heads are full of preconceived and irrelevant notions. The mammoth truths of marriage and family are all in their accustomed lairs. But we will find them only in the old, patient way: by watching the principal water holes, by gauging the height of the grass along their trails, and by plodding in the tracks of their feet.

The exegetical method therefore—the back-to-the-books approach—has its difficulties. To drop all the fancy imagery, the main problem is that old books are hard to read. They don't ring many bells the first six times through, and since most people have trouble finishing one reading, that's about where it ends. There are some advantages, however. For those with the eyes for small print, no allergy to dust, and enough discipline to keep reading *until* they comprehend, instead of stopping when they don't, the job is pretty straightforward. All they have to do is live with the old stuff. Not of course with a view to copying it in this day and age—we shot that canard in the last chapter—but in order to acquire the veteran hunter's eye and ear, by the simple device of running into the beast over and over again in all sorts of places. Read St. Paul till you break through his almost impenetrable prose; read the old marriage rite till you are its contemporary; watch people like Nicholas Farrar at Little Gidding or Thomas More singing with his family; listen to Augustine *On the Conjugal Good* or Eric Gill on sex, to Jeremy Taylor on *The*

Marriage Ring or William Law on Paternus and Eusebia; and keep at it until the horse sense that makes them ageless breaks through the oddness that makes them antique. It is a tough job, and the devil has seen to it that most of the books are either out of print or mighty unattractive. But it's the best of all possible ways to work. At the end of it—before the end of it, in fact, but unfortunately not too close to the beginning of it—you will start to acquire a taste for hunting and a nose for elephants. You will begin to find elephants the way elephants find elephants. You will become an insider, an expert in your own right, and you will not be fooled anymore by the blind guides that keep trying to sell you their services. It is worth all the eyestrain and nodding over dull pages you have to put into it.

For out of it the real subjects will begin to show up in person. You will not have to go through life listening to Adjustment tell you he is more important than Initiative, or hearing Security insist that Maturity yield him place. All the pseudo-subjects will finally shut up and sit down and, ever so gradually but ever so surely, What It's Really About will begin to dawn. You will start with mute and awkward stones, great blocks to be laid course by course, and by hand: Man, Husband, Father; Woman, Wife, Mother; Bed, Board, Bread, Wine. But you will slowly begin to see what it is that is being built, the Great Mystery behind all these pieces. It is nothing less than the forming of our discreteness and separateness into a created reflection of the coinherence of God. It is humanity disclosing itself as the image of the Trinity. It is the Mystical Body, the City of God: real individuals in real roles, really meant to find themselves through their membership in each other. And that is the Real Thing. That is the bus on which History is only an employee, and Maturity only a little hot air in the tires. It's you and I for whom it was chartered.

As I said, though, the method has its difficulties. And out here in the cold courtyard around the fire it is not very realistic. My only copy of Augustine is in Latin. I had to give Jeremy Taylor's sermons back to the monastery library from which I filched them and the only Eric Gill I had was borrowed but never returned. Accordingly, despite its merits, exegesis isn't going to work. What is left for us therefore is simply to join hands, and to begin casting about with what light we have. How many of the real foundation stones of the City of God we will be able to pick up this way is anybody's guess. At the very least, we can keep each other company.

WHEN YOU LOOK AROUND for the absolutely first course of blocks in the subject of matrimony there is only one possible choice. In order to be a father, a husband, a wife, a mother—you still have to begin by being a man or a woman. Therefore it is the vocation to be human that has to come first of all. This is one of the most obvious elephants around, yet we almost always miss it. If marriage is the great mystery of the City, the image of the Coinherence—if we do indeed become members one of another in it—then there is obviously going to be a fundamental need in marriage for people to be able to get along with each other and with themselves. And that is precisely what the rules of human behavior are about. They are concerned with the mortaring of the joints of the City, with the strengthening of the ligatures of the Body. The moral laws are not just a collection of arbitrary parking regulations invented by God to make life complicated; they are the only way for human nature to be natural.

For example, I am told not to lie because in the long run lying destroys my own, and my neighbor's, nature. And the same goes for murder and envy, obviously; for gluttony and sloth, not quite so obviously; and for lust and pride not very obviously at all, but just as truly. Marriage is natural, and it demands the fullness of nature if it is to be itself. But *human* nature. And human nature in one piece, not in twenty-three self-frustrating fragments. A man and a woman schooled in pride cannot simply sit down together and start caring. It takes humility to look wide-eyed at somebody else, to praise, to cherish, to honor. They will have to acquire some before they can succeed. For as long as it lasts, of course, the first throes of romantic love will usually extort it from them, but when the initial wonder fades and familiarity begins to hobble biology, it's going to take virtue to bring it off.

Again, a husband and a wife cannot long exist as one flesh, if they are habitually unkind, rude or untruthful. Every sin breaks down the body of the Mystery, puts asunder what God and nature have joined. The marriage rite is aware of this; it binds us to loving, to honoring, to cherishing, for just that reason. This is all obvious in the extreme, but it needs saying loudly and often. The only available candidates for matrimony are, every last one of them, sinners. As sinners, they are in a fair way to wreck themselves and anyone else who gets within arm's length of them. Without virtue, therefore, no marriage will make it. The first of all vocations, the ground line of the walls of the New Jerusalem is made of stuff like truthfulness, patience, love and liberality; of prudence, justice, temperance and courage; and of all their adjuncts and circumstances: manners, consideration, fair speech and the ability to keep one's mouth shut and one's heart open, as needed.

And since this is all so utterly necessary and so highly likely to be in short supply at the crucial moments, it isn't going to be enough to deliver earnest exhortations to uprightness and stalwartness. The parties to matrimony should be prepared for its being, on numerous occasions, no party at all; they should be instructed that they will need both forgiveness and forgivingness if they are to survive the festivities. Neither virtue, nor the ability to forgive the absence of virtue, are about to force their presence on us, and therefore we ought to be loudly and frequently forewarned that only the grace of God is sufficient to keep nature from coming unstuck. Fallen man does not rise by his own efforts; there is no balm in Gilead. Our domestic ills demand an imported remedy.

~∞~

THE REST OF THAT SUBJECT is my regular business. I shall not get into it here. I press on to the second course of blocks. Again, it is obvious. So much so that it is the source of half the jokes in the world. It was not enough for the Creator to make us human. Absurdly, he went further. Male and Female created he them. The truth of our being is that we are one species, but just barely. Even without counting porpoises, this planet houses two different sorts of rationality, two different kinds of freedom, and two different brands of love: men's and women's. But nowhere else are we more confused about our roles than we are in the matter of sexuality. Chesterton once said, "About sex especially men are born mad; and they hardly reach sanity until they reach sanctity." Sex, therefore, rears its ugly head.

Do you know why it is ugly? Because it is unreal. There *is* such a thing as sexuality. In grammar it is called gender. It is the word used to describe the marvelous bargain by which we get two species for the price of one. But there is no such real thing as sex. It is an ersatz third thing, existing only in the mind. It is neither masculine nor feminine, and ultimately it is destructive of any true concept of sexuality. Do you want me to prove it? Listen.

Suppose I wrote a book called *The Sexual Life of a Nun*. You know what people would think. They would be curious—or shocked. They would expect to find it either a big joke or a compilation of slightly prurient propaganda. How many would be able to see that, on the real meaning of the word *sexual*, it is a perfectly proper title? For a nun's life of course is utterly sexual. She thinks as a woman, prays as a woman, reacts as a woman and commits herself as a woman. No monk, no celibate, ever embraced his life for her kind of reasons. He couldn't if he wanted to. Of course she omits, as an offering to God, one particular expression of her sexuality; but it is only one out of a hundred. The sexual congress she does not attend is not life's most important meeting, all the marriage manuals to the contrary notwithstanding.

Accordingly, Sex is the villain of our little piece here. It has eclipsed true sexuality as religiosity sometimes swallows up religion, that is, as an unreal subject that makes it impossible for people to see the real one. We are full of Sex, more so day by day. And at the same time we grow progressively emptier of masculinity and femininity. The fundamental division of the species is the one about which we have the least to say. The abstractness of the male intellect, the concreteness of the female, the man's characteristic grasp of the whole and the woman's typical attention to the part, his minding of the bank balance and hers of the children's need for underwear—all these things we can make nothing of except to fight over them. Instead of pursuing them, of refining and purifying them, we only let them rattle around without supervision, and wonder why we do not know each other better. We settle for living separate lives, interrupted occasionally by a short confrontation between the sheets, in which we are so busy thinking about Sex that we have no time to think about being men or women. Except for bed, courtship, and affairs, we can make nothing of the opposite sex. From birth to twelve, and from twenty till death, we gather in separate groups, on opposite sides of the room, until some dolt decides to liven up the party by playing round games, and embarrasses us all with our ignorance of the other half of the race.

∽෨∾

THE NEXT COURSE OF STONES takes us above ground level. So far the roles have had nothing specifically to do with marriage. They have been only the raw materials out of which marriages are made. Now it is time for the functions we acquire by marriage itself. And the first are Husband and Wife.

As you might expect, the confusion over sexuality causes more trouble in this department than in any other. Sex as a mythical third thing is irrelevant to the actualities of either sex, but it is more irrelevant to women. For while it is not like masculinity in any real sense, it does contain more detached masculine elements than feminine ones, and when it is applied indiscriminately to both sexes, it tends to be harder on women—to saddle them with a number of highly inconvenient masculine ideals. For example:

Sex, as commonly conceived, is something a couple *do* together. But the sexual act itself is not quite like that. It is, and remains, something a man does to a woman. They are not both working at the same thing. He is giving, she is receiving. He is the lover, she the beloved. Now, if they both set out to "have some Sex," the whole delicate balance is wrecked, and neither can find his own role. What is happening is that the *difference* we all love so dearly is taking a bad beating. The wife is being backed into a decreasingly feminine role, even in overtly sexual matters, and the husband is finding that he has less and less of an object to be masculine toward. He is getting what he wants, but not what he needs. He asks frequently enough, but has lost sight of what to ask for; and that is deadly. We are already far madder on the subject of sex than we ought to be; guilt breathes down our necks in this department oftener than in any other. What a shame, then, in the one place where, as Augustine saith, concupiscence can be subjugated to reason, or as we might say, sex can become sane, we so easily swallow the propaganda that has made Sex a dirty word. For it is just that. Sexuality isn't. Intercourse isn't, bed isn't and pleasure isn't; but *Sex* is. Dirty and irrelevant. Only the empty-headed and the utterly deluded among us can have failed to grasp that.

Incidentally, there is a key here to why husbands and wives, on not infrequent occasions, seek beds other than their own. Affairs are generally either roundly condemned or extravagantly praised. Neither attitude is quite appropriate, but there is some truth in each. The condemnation is deserved because an affair is of necessity either the impossible undertaking of a parallel commitment, or a deliberate attempt to escape from one exclusive vow into another. There isn't much to choose between them. But the praise, while not deserved, is not as out of place as mere morality would seem to say. In an affair, it is precisely the real roles of Man and Woman, of Lover and Beloved, that are temporarily, if impossibly, restored. For as long as it stays fresh, the thing constitutes a restoration of the relation of courtship, and people respond to it mightily. He feels like a man for the first time in years; she rejoices to find someone who will treat her as a woman. It gets pretty corny after that, but it's true just the same. It's a good thing to remember the next time you try to talk somebody out of an affair. You can't excuse it, and you shouldn't palliate it, but don't make the mistake of telling them there's nothing to it. Quite apart from love and friendship, the mere restoration to masculinity and femininity for a few hours a week is enough of an attraction to keep the thing going for a good while.

But back to the marriage bed. St. Paul may have been prejudiced toward women (what with not letting them speak in church), and we may be able to sit loose to his *obiter dicta* about them; but on the subject of wives and husbands he deserves more of a hearing than he currently gets. The husband, he says, is the head of the wife, just as Christ is the head of the Church. The marriage rite takes him at his word. It is the groom who speaks first, gives first and loves first. The bride is to obey, to receive and to respond. (Let me anticipate an objection. The word *obey*. I know it isn't in the American version of the rite. It was hacked out in 1892 by one of those periodic committees of revising do-gooders who would cut out our hearts if they thought it would make us up-to-date. They wreck a lot of fine old scenery and every now and then they throw out an old truth along with an archaic verb form, but they don't do too much real harm. The word obey isn't in the marriage vow anymore, but the whole of St. Paul's glorious passage on marriage and the Mystical Body is in the epistle for the nuptial Mass—complete with the duty of wives to submit to their husbands. So St. Paul got even with them after all. They can't win, but they never stop trying.)

The reason the headship of the husband is so violently objected to is that it is misunderstood. First of all, St. Paul's anti-feminist prejudices notwithstanding, the Bible does not say that *men* and *women* are unequal. Neither does the Church. There are no second-class citizens in the New Jerusalem. It is *husbands* and *wives* that are unequal. It is precisely in marriage (a state, you will recall, not to be continued as such in heaven) that they enter into a relationship of superior to inferior—of head to body. And the difference there is not one of worth, ability or intelligence, but of *role*. It is functional, not organic. It is based on the exigencies of the Dance, not on a judgment as to talent. In the ballet, in any intricate dance, one dancer leads, the other follows. Not because one is better (he may or may not be), but because that is his part. Our mistake, here as elsewhere, is to think that equality and diversity are unreconcilable. The common notion of equality is based on the image of the march. In a parade, really unequal beings are dressed alike, given guns of identical length, trained to hold them at the same angle, and ordered to keep step with a fixed beat. But it is not the parade that is true to life; it is the dance. There you have real equals assigned unequal roles in order that each may achieve his individual perfection in the whole. Nothing is less personal than a parade; nothing more so than a dance. It is the choice image of fulfillment through function, and it comes very close to the heart of the Trinity. Marriage is a hierarchical game played by co-equal persons. Keep that paradox and you move in the freedom of the Dance; alter it, and you grow weary with marching.

But that only says what the headship doesn't mean. What it does mean is equally misunderstood. The husband is over his wife as the head is over the body. It isn't a description of what ought to be; it just says what it *is*. He *is* the head. He will be a good one or a bad one, depending; but if he isn't the head, there isn't any other. He is to be the lover, she the beloved. If he doesn't initiate, she will wither of neglect. She cannot supply what only he can give. If the locomotive doesn't pull, the train doesn't move.

He, then, is to love and cherish her. And he is to do it first, because he promised it first. She must do it too, of course, but in her own way, as an answering voice, a

49

counterpoint. Unfortunately it doesn't often work out that way. And our little bête noire, Sex, doesn't help much. One of the commonest ways it succeeds in frustrating honest sexuality is to train men to look on women as sources of stimulation, rather than as objects of love. They come to marriage after years of being conditioned to respond to certain more or less irrelevant fetishes—the height of heels, the length of hair, the size of waistlines, the prominence of busts. When they become husbands, however, they find that what they have learned to consider Sexy is not too dependably supplied by marriage. Waistlines thicken as the years go by, and busts fall and fashions change. But husbands still wait to be aroused, and not infrequently they wait more than they do anything else. They grow impatient. They complain. If, in their disgruntlement, they resort to reading marriage books, they are liable to get the impression that the source of the trouble is lack of technique: theirs, if they are diffident; their wives', if they are arrogant. But that isn't the trouble at all. It's that they are being passive where they should be active. Don't misunderstand. Perhaps most husbands *do* fairly well. The point is that what they are doing is responding, not leading, and their wives suffer for it. No human being can afford to settle for being only the *occasion* of somebody else's pleasure. No wife can long endure being treated as if her chief sexual function were to arouse her husband. That puts the shoe on exactly the wrong foot. She is, after all, a person; if her husband never grows from passion and response into action and love—if he doesn't stop waiting to be aroused and realize he's got to make something of a career of arousing—she is not going to find being a wife much of a fulfillment.

As a priest, I listen dutifully to a lot of wifely discontent. Women have their faults, and I don't suppose there is a pastor on earth who doesn't at times wish he had the power to convert them all back into ribs—nice, quiet, uncomplaining ribs. But all this female smoldering is evidence of a fire somewhere. I dare say that at least one of its causes is the failure of their husbands to treat them as wives—to be indeed their heads, their lovers and their first movers. An appalling number of men are relational blanks in their marriages. Maybe now and then—in bed—a husband acquires some color, some substance, in his wife's eyes, but too often that's the only place. All or nothing. She receives no *minor* sexual attention. The adjunct daily affections—the little passes executed only because he wills them, not because he is aroused—these she does not see. The cajolery and fair speech, the gallantry and unconsummated buffoonery that is man—these she never gets. She has no head. She has only one more tired member who has to be caught in a good mood and worked up.

Small wonder, then, that wives do such unwifely things. No marvel that there are so many active trousered women to make up for passive trousered men. As a matter of fact, we have become the trousered race, not the human race. There is only one sex left, and that is: Sex. And while both wives and husbands are responsible for the debacle, it is husbands who have done the most damage, and it is they who can, if they will, do the most good. If the train doesn't move, repair the locomotive. Don't let the cars sit around blaming themselves for not being engines. Above all, don't let them try to act as if they were. For the cars have their own function, they are what the train is really *about*. They are what the engine is *for*. All the space in a husband is supposed to be given over to providing traction; it is the wife's capacity for freight that makes the trip worthwhile. The comparison is hardly flattering, but it does manage to be a bit gallant and, as a husband, I am rather pleased that I was able to get it off. One should try to practice what one preaches, with or without elegance.

HUSBAND AND WIFE, however, are only the beginning of the hierarchy. Under normal conditions, involvement in matrimony means entering something like what scientists call a critical state. The situation, not to mention the wife, becomes pregnant with possibilities. And when those possibilities are actualized they begin to require minding and feeding, they conduct interminable conversations on the telephone, they borrow cars, get into scrapes and generally cause their parents to wonder what it was they could possibly have had in mind. The happy couple have let themselves in for Fatherhood and Motherhood, and it is the unvarnished irreversibility of those vocations that brings us to the next course of stones.

Here again, the building up of the Body, the fruition of the Mystery, operates through the divine comedy of hierarchy among equals. Here again—this time as parents and children—human beings of equal worth, but with diverse functions, are set in a dance in order that their separateness might become membership in each other. Here again, persons are invited into the Coinherence through love. And here again, it is the man who is the head. Not ought to be; *is*. For good or for ill.

We are perhaps less confused about our roles as fathers and mothers than about husbandhood and wifehood, but confused we still are, and one of the principal features of our befuddlement as husbands and wives come across here with no change: We are vaguer about fatherhood than motherhood. Mommy may have her problems, but Daddy is very nearly useless. And that is both sad and unnatural. When the authors of Scripture looked around for an image with which to explain the divine love—when the Holy Ghost finally ratified the choice of a name for the Very First Person of the Godhead—it was Father. Mother was not neglected; we have the Blessed Mother, Mother Church, and Jerusalem, the Mother of us all. But it was Father who took the highest honors. Now, however, we have only Mother's Day and Father's Day, and while there isn't much to choose between them, Mother's Day does at least manage to retain a few shreds of intelligibility. Father's Day is a joke, and a commercially motivated one at that. If you want to prove the poverty of our knowledge about fatherhood, go out next June and buy a half-dozen "serious" Father's Day cards. They are good for more laughs than all the funny ones put together—provided they don't bring you to the verge of tears first. You will find corn, cuteness and can't, but you won't come within a hundred miles of that masterpiece of nature after whom God himself was named. Where in the midst of all that sincere sentiment will you find the features of Abraham, Isaac and Jacob? The Patriarch is an impossible concept to us—anyone who is due more than socks, neckties and tobacco is inconceivable. Where is the Teacher of sons and daughters? Fathers are told they do little besides harm; we hire psychiatrists to straighten out the havoc they leave behind them. And where is the Priest, the Offerer, the Interceder, the Mediator; where is the Judge, the Guardian of the Law? All we see are ciphers, who occasionally manage to whip themselves into being Pals.

As always, it is easier to stigmatize than to prescribe. And it is harder still to cure. I know. I am a father, and on a fairly wholesale basis. The critical fowling piece I unlimbered in the last paragraph points at me as well as at the rest of the world. With the single exception of the fact that I do not receive neckties, every one of those shots goes home hard. Oh, I try. Maybe more than a lot of others. Wholesale example to the flock of Christ, and all that. But I am a long way from where I ought to be, and so are most of the men whom I know to be trying and admire for it. First off, because of vices. Other men have the same problems. In place of my short temper or laziness, they may have coldness or favoritism, but very few of us get anywhere near par for the course, and the honest ones among us know it. But with equal honesty we know that this is not the heart of the problem; it will always be with us, and while it must be resisted, it has to be more or less expected. The root of the trouble is the same old blindness as before: We cannot see our roles anymore.

I'm afraid I don't have much to say. In no other instance am I more frantically hunting elephants than in this one. Mostly, I guess, I actually do what I started out saying we can't do. I copy the old chromos. I am an anachronism. While I lecture at my dinner table, while I admonish my children, while I rule, while I judge, I listen with half an ear. I sound like something out of Clarence Day. The only thing I can comfort myself with is that maybe, out of it all, I will come up with one or two good up-to-date adaptations. Outside of that, I have only bits and pieces. Like these scraps of advice to myself on the subject of children.

Be their Teacher. And expect a lot from them. Avoid, of course, the mistake of demanding they learn things you don't give a hang about. They see right through that why-don't-you-go-find-a-hobby bit. But if you're honestly wild about math or letters, music or shopwork, give them both barrels and make them sit still for it. They will gripe and you will get grouchy, but if you *really* love it, something will rub off that will stay with them like the smell of fresh bread. So don't be afraid to demand your kind of stuff of them. They aren't going to see that many people who *care*. It would be nice if their father could be one. It would be something to hold in their hands all their lives.

Be their Lover. Give yourself, your humor, your small talk, and the minor affections of your hands and eyes. Don't keep it all in the solemn now-let's-you-and-Daddy-talk-about-your-report-card vein. Give them the best of your offhand style. Let your sons grow up learning what a man who acts out his caring looks like. Let your daughters learn what it's like to have a man around who works at quickening their response. It might just pay off in a decent son-in-law.

Be a just Judge. Children can stand vast amounts of sternness. They rather expect to be wrong; and they are quite used to being punished. It is injustice, inequity and inconsistency that kill them. Fathers, provoke not your children to wrath, lest they be disheartened. It is precisely the sight of injustice that triggers anger, and it is precisely the helpless rage of inferiors that takes the heart out of them and produces most of the cynics, skeptics and smart alecks in the world. You are first of all the Guardians of the Law. Develop a passion for fairness. If you overdo anything, make it that.

One more. *Delight in them openly.* Speak your praise of them. Be their Priest. Look at them with the widest eyes you can manage, and don't be ashamed to be seen at wonder. You will not see their like again. What a shame if they should leave without ever knowing they have been beheld and offered up by an astonished heart.

All in all, though, the main thing I know about fatherhood is that it comes at us so thick and so fast that maybe even knowing what to do wouldn't quite turn the trick. And if I am in the dark here, where I have the benefit of on-the-job training, I am even more benighted about motherhood. Nevertheless, there is a spark or two to be struck.

To be a Mother is to be the sacrament—the effective symbol—of *place*. Mothers do not *make* homes, they *are* our home: in the simple sense that we begin our days by a long sojourn within the body of a woman; in the extended sense that she remains our center of gravity through the years. She is the very diagram of belonging, the *where* in whose vicinity we are fed and watered, and have our wounds bound up and our noses wiped. She is geography incarnate, with her breasts and her womb, her relative immobility, and her hands reaching up to us the fruitfulness of the earth. All this is no doubt a bit remote now, what with Mother out at a job, and all the nursing bottles and packaged bread hard at work to hide her from our sight—but fortunately the circumstances of her role are such that she is not nearly as ignorant of it as Father is of his. Though she bakes packaged mixes, she still bakes; though she no longer spins and weaves, she still clothes and mends; though she is surrounded by machinery to do her work, she herself still moves in the old orbit: from sink to stove to store, and round and round again. And all this is a great mercy. Her function forces itself upon her.

Therefore there is a difference between the derelictions

of fathers and mothers. The trouble with us as fathers is that it is too easy for us to escape our roles. Nothing of fatherhood is physically forced upon us, and so nothing is just about what we do—we are functional blanks. That cannot fairly be said of women. But what can be said of them is that while they do fulfill their functions, they are increasingly tempted to do so for the wrong reason. They are led, subtly but surely, to look on the mothering they do as mere necessity—even a penance—and they live as if they were reserving their real enthusiasm for something else, usually unspecified. They list themselves apologetically as "only a mother"; and they accumulate endless labor-saving devices, in order to conserve themselves for some other and better role than motherhood. The labor-saving devices of course are a trap. More often than not, they simply make more work; and what time they do save is usually devoured by the car and the TV. But occasionally the other role does materialize. Women go to work; sometimes simply to find fulfillment, sometimes on the basis of real necessity; but often only to get more money to buy more devices to spare themselves for more work. Yet in few cases do they work at anything worth saving themselves for. They plough through their motherly functions every day—most of them do fabulously well; they are a remarkable breed—but then they escape for fulfillment to some bit of ten-to-four clerking or six-to-twelve piecework that is less fulfilling than making instant chocolate pudding. The really dreadful part of it all is the wear and tear; for by definition, and by choice, they are not substituting one function for another, but acting two roles on the strength of only one small heart.

Now at this point, I am perilously close to looking for the elephant where I have said I mustn't. It's beginning to sound like one of the usual pleas to send women back to *Kinder, Küche, und Kirche*. But not quite. There is a principle. The mother is the geographical center of her family, the body out of whom their diversity springs, the neighborhood in which that diversity begins ever so awkwardly to dance its way back to the true Body which is the Mother of us all. Her role then is precisely to be there for them. Not necessarily over there, but just *there*—*thereness itself*, if you will; not necessarily *in* her place but *place itself* to them; not necessarily *at* home but *home itself*. It sounds pretty abstruse, but at least it's a lead that doesn't automatically go straight back to the old chromo of the three K's. Of course in most cases that is where it will lead. It may well be that of all the roles in marriage, motherhood is the one least ill at ease with the old patterns. A man playing *Life with Father* at his own table is ludicrous; a woman kneading bread is still lovely. In the case of motherhood, there is a great deal to be said for trying on the old hats first. They might look funny, and it is a woman's privilege not to wear them; but she should at least try them on—and work them over for a while. A few snips here and a bit of ribbon there, and some of them can be as stunning as ever.

But in the rarer cases the principle may lead elsewhere than to the kneading trough. I say rarer. A lot of women talk as if they would be writing the great American novel if it weren't for their mothering. Well, maybe. But it would mean a lot more novels than one could reasonably expect. And it would mean a lot more discipline in the women. For every woman who is really stymied in her creativity by the received patterns of family life, there are six who only think they are. There are swans and there are geese; and they themselves are welcome to the job of deciding who's who. When they do, the geese, all humble and uncomplaining, should go back to the kitchen, and stop faking; and the swans should shut up about how hard it is and start flying. If anyone is going to be able to come up with a reconciliation of motherhood and career, they are. Let them take the principle, then, and work out the new patterns that will get it off the ground.

I have only a couple of practical suggestions for the swans.

The first is: Don't burn the kneading trough yet. As a working mother, or a mother with a career, you certainly won't use it often. But remember, you are a landmark. From time to time—of an evening, at Easter—you will do well to appear in your old place and shape. You are and remain the bodily link with our origin. You are the oldest thing in the world; don't be in a hurry to forget any of your history.

The second comes out of that. You are not only a link with something. You are the *thing* itself; and you are the sacrament, the instrument, by which we learn to love the things that are. Your body is the first object any child of man ever wanted. Therefore dispose yourself to be loved, to be wanted, to be available. Be *there* for them with a vengeance. Be a gracious, bending woman. Incline your ear, your heart, your hands to them. Be found warm and comfortable, and disposed to affection. Be ready to be done by and to welcome their casual effusions with something better than preoccupation and indifference. It isn't a matter of how much time; only how much intensity. Children love fat mothers. They like them because while any mother is a diagram of *place*, a picture of *home*, a fat one is a clearer diagram, a greater sacrament. She is more *there*. I can think of no better wish to all the slender swans of this present age than to propose them a toast: May your husbands find you as slim as they like; your children should always remember you were fat.

And with that unflattering but sincere outburst I have just shot my wad on the subject. The great truth is that we exist for our functions, not our functions for us. I was not put here to get myself happy, but to put myself into my role. It's somebody else's job to look after me. I'm supposed to be too busy with my own work to have time. We don't often do it that way, but that is how we are put together.

V

BED

A geography of matrimony; with two maps and a careful but inconclusive discussion of one of the principal quagmires.

B UT THE FUNCTIONS ARE NOT THE WHOLE STORY. *Things* enter into marriage as well as persons. The Holy Estate of Matrimony is a highly material proposition. It takes *place*, at *times*, and is thoroughly tied down to the particularities of a bodily world. It's all very well to talk about the roles of the dancers and the need to know them better, but the dancers' movements are defined as much by the shape of the stage as by their parts. Life is not a series of abstract designs, of elegant plans and outlines, but a headlong stumbling through real valleys full of historic potholes. Therefore it's not enough simply to know the goal of the journey, nor even the nature of the travelers: Knowledge of the terrain is essential. Hardware and geography enter into the essence of marriage.

In premarital instructions, as part of the effort to focus attention on what really matters, I usually say that you need only two things, two pieces of matter, to make a home: a bed and a table. It's an oversimplification, but it's a good one—it comes close to being a diagram. For Bed and Board are the fundamental geographical divisions of the family; they are the chief places, and it is in them, at them and around them that we dance the parts we are given. More, they are boundaries that mark the areas of our freedom in marriage. It is precisely the confines of the stage that render the dancers' freedom effective: The ballet is saved from enslavement to limitless idea by the lights in front and the drops in back. The graceful flight up the curving staircase, the pursuit, the capture, the embrace, are delivered from being mere concepts, delivered into the real world—delivered as a child is delivered—by the very solidity of the stairs, by the precise height of the risers and the depth of the treads. Geography snatches them from the edge of the boundless void and defines them into freedom. And so marriage is delivered by the bed. The untamability of romance, the endlessness of the vision of the beloved, threaten constantly to send us off in successive limitless expeditions after something that grows successively harder to define. The movie star on her fifth marriage seems always to be less clear about what she wants and less free to make her wanting serve her well. For under it all lies the endlessly expansive pride of a being who cannot add a cubit to her stature or a minute to her life. That is our dilemma: desire is endless; we are not. Listen.

And the Lord God said, Behold, the man is become as one of us, to know good and evil; the unexpansible is expanding. *And now, lest he put forth his hand, and take also of the tree of life, and eat, and live forever*; lest he use grace and freedom only to confirm his breach with nature; *therefore the Lord God sent him forth from the garden of Eden…and he placed…Cherubims, and a flaming sword which turned every way, to keep the way of the tree of life.* And so Adam goes out to his land of thorns and thistles, and Eve to her bed of conception and birth, precisely to be saved by geography, to be restored by the tilling of the ground, to become more than dust by returning to dust, to be defined by being confined.

All this the marriage rite knows. Marriage was instituted in the time of man's innocency, but it has operated ever since under the shadow of the fall. Therefore its materialities, along with all our other materialities, become the means of our cure. He who perished by a tree is saved by a tree. He who died by an apple is restored by eating the flesh of his Saviour. Our lust is to be healed by being brought down to one bed, our savagery tamed by the exchanges around a lifelong table. Bed, Board, rooftree and doorway become the choice places of our healing, the delimitations of our freedom. By setting us boundaries, they hold us in; but they trammel the void as well. By confining, they keep track of us—they leave us free to be found, and to find ourselves. The vow of lifelong fidelity to one bed, one woman, becomes the wall at the edge of the cliff that leaves the children free to play a little, rather than be lost at large. Marriage gives us somewhere to *be*.

I said before, you can't hide an elephant. Unfortunately, it's even harder to hide a theologian. I apologize for this excursion, but not very abjectly. I make no promises about reforming.

I shall get to the Board and its adjuncts by and by. Table and rooftree, nursery and kitchen, even patio and rumpus room, will all have their turn. But the first must come first, and that is the Bed: the couple's initial piece of real estate. The things that come later in a marriage are, one way or another, extensions of this—added parcels, adjacent lots, buffer strips and subdivisions. The bed itself is their first soil, the uncrossed plain waiting for boundary and marker, for plough and seed. If this is well laid and planted, the rest will have order and comeliness; if not, they will be senseless bits of gerrymandering, spreading far and wide for reasons that have nothing to do with the good of the people of the land. The bed is the heart of home, the arena of love, the seedbed of life, and the one constant point of meeting. It is the place where, night by night, forgiveness and fair speech return that the sun go not down upon our wrath; where the perfunctory kiss and the entirely ceremonial pat on the backside become unction and grace. It is the oldest, friendliest thing in anybody's marriage, the first used and the last left, and no one can praise it enough.

But there is mystery in it too. It is a strange piece of terrain, and finding ourselves in it is as unlikely as it is marvelous. We marry on attack or rebound. We come at each other for an assortment of pretty thin and transitory reasons. We ask, and are taken in matrimony; and in the haste of charge or retreat, we find ourselves thrown down into a very small piece of ground indeed. The marriage bed is a trench; adversity has made us bedfellows. I turn over at night. I try to see where I am and who is with me. It is not what I imagined at all. Where are the two triumphant giants of love I expected, where the conqueror smiling at conqueror? There are only the two of us, crouched down here under a barrage of years, bills and petty grievances, waiting for a signal which shows no sign of coming. Most likely we shall die in this trench. There is really no place else to go, so in the meantime we talk to each other. The sum and substance of what we manage to say, however, is "Well, here we are."

We have come to a calamitous involvement. What are we doing here, in position ridiculous, at pleasure transitory, with results disastrous? What will we not cause? What consequences to self and others? Indeed, what others will we not cause? Children! Independent beings to go forth to their own births, involvements and deaths; to love, to skin their knees, to have their hearts broken, and to lie in other trenches, distant but not different from this. I am Abraham. I pick up the knife and fire when I beget. This bed, this trench, is cut *across* my line of march. I can crawl along it, but not past it. It is a lateral passage, a byroad to Mount Moriah, a side trip into terror. All the rosy marriage books about the joys of procreation, all the neat, even true, theological niceties about its being my share in the creative process, leave me literally cold—with fear and trembling. The only comfort is my first comfort—that it is absurd and therefore sane. In terms of its actual results—in the real and logical framework in which all such treatments try to put it—it remains insoluble, absurd, the square root of -1. It is only when taken as insoluble, and when put into another framework, that it begins to give answers. I am not being obscure; let me say at once, in plain English, what that framework is. It is the Cross of Christ, where God Incarnate works to reconcile the broken and dishonored fragments of the City by being himself broken and dishonored. If I were not invited into that mystery, I do not think I could afford to be honest about what a calamity we are all in. Only Christian marriage has a real chance to save nature. Not that mine is very natural—it can't be, because it isn't very Christian; but the truth remains. The disciple is not above his master; the Cross is foolishness, and the marriage bed is absurd. That much rings true. So far, so good.

Kierkegaard said all this pretty well. He had the honesty to admit that he was scared and couldn't find the answers. Read him if you want more on absurdity. But read *him*, not too many of his commentators. They will leave you cold—for lack of fear and trembling. They make absurdity into a higher good, and that is the one thing you can't do with it. Turn it into a mystique and you reduce it to one more logical gimmick that doesn't fit. Read him, then, till you realize that all you will ever get is the command from nowhere to sacrifice Isaac. And read St. Paul again. We lie down in marriage with the weakness of God and the foolishness of the Cross, and the invitation to affirm the whole thing by faith. A lot of people reason their way out of the conjugal bed, but no one in his right mind reasons his way into it. It is a calamitous involvement indeed. Only an equally calamitous commitment can bring it off.

The bed, then, is both light and dark, fertile upland and beleaguered trench. Now anything that big is going to be hard to grasp in one piece, and it is precisely the inadequacy of their grasp that makes most of the comments on it unreal. But there are a couple of them that are worth the time of anybody's day, and as you might suspect, they are in the old places. The first is the traditional list of the three ends of marriage found now in the rite of the Church of England and also in the Latin originals. Marriage, the priest tells the company present, was instituted for the procreation of children, for a remedy against sin, and for mutual society, help and comfort. The second is the priceless sentence with which, in the same rite, the groom gives the ring to his bride: With this ring I thee wed, with my body I thee worship, with all my worldly goods I thee endow, in the name of the Father and of the Son and of the Holy Ghost. (Once again the bowdlerizers have put their sticky fingers into the pie. Every smitch of this, with the exception of "With this ring I thee wed" and the invocation of the name of God has been chopped out of the American Prayer Book. I don't know how they missed what they left. Oh, such dreadful, well-meaning revisers—committees composed of equal numbers of liberal higher critics and Victorian spinsters. Between the two of them they managed to remove a good many of the heights and most of the depths of the rite. The critics took care of Significance: Adam and Eve, Isaac and Rebekah, Abraham and Sarah all went down under the same hatchet; the spinsters finished off Spice: The body's worship was just too much for their nasty-nice sensibilities. Someday we will put it all back, to serve them, and us, right. The Church is a peasant with her feet on solid earth where they belong. She will never look right up on a lecture platform trying to hide her old hat just because it isn't stylish.)

Taken together anyway, these two old formularies lay hold of the full width of even the widest bed. What a marvelous set of measurements they are. They begin with an accurate statement of the most calamitous of all the bed's results—children. Procreation comes first on the list. Next, they take seriously the idea of marriage as a remedy against sin, and isn't that a strange one now? We don't talk much anymore about lust as a disease. We don't see ourselves as imperiled by fornication; instead we name it Sex and praise it to the skies; but a disease it is nonetheless, and marrying remains its cure. Sex teaches me to desire all women above a very low passing grade. Marriage gives me only one. If it's Sex I'm after, the conjugal bed is not much of an improvement over celibacy. The result of it all is that we enjoy our beds for a while, and after that, we grumble. The one thing we don't do is take the treatment full force. Don't think we do. We would be a lot healthier than we are if we did. Our bodies may be in it, but our minds and eyes are too often elsewhere to let us be cured. And then there is the last of the three purposes: mutual society, help and comfort. It is the most palatable of the old ideas: Everybody agrees with it, takes it for granted, and promptly loses sight of it, sometimes for years on end. We were meant to meet, to sustain and to ease each other, and in the marriage bed we lie down to do just that. It is an island in a sea of troubles, where there is nothing else to do but rest and refresh. Yet how resourceful we are, with our turned backs and stubborn silences, or with our interminable pouts and dreadful debates about What's Wrong With Us.

And then take the main item in the ring bestowal: With my body I thee worship. A man can give his wife so little besides trouble. He makes a life of hard labor for her, preempts most of her available time by begetting children upon her, and then leaves her alone with the whole business for the greater part of every working day. It is precisely the worship of his body for her that she so badly needs and so seldom gets. And from an occasionally aroused husband she will never have it, though she wait a hundred years. That can come only from a worshipful spouse who works at his devotions with discipline and perseverance. People admit it's hard to pray. Yet they think

71

it's easy to make love. What nonsense. Neither is worth much when it is only the outcropping of intermittent enthusiasm. Both need to be done without ceasing; and that puts a premium on the minor manifestations. Obviously the sexual act itself is central. But the circle that is drawn around it consists of a thousand small passes and light touches. What they lack in moment they more than make up for by sheer weight of numbers, and it is a poor bed that sees only the grand piece of business that really arrives. It is precisely the unconsummated nonsense that makes the main absurdity fruitful. Sexual intercourse is indeed *society* (though often not too mutual), and it is certainly a *comfort*, when it goes well; but it is seldom much *help* unless its disastrousness is softened by a vast amount of incidental tenderness.

That will do, I think, for the list. Perhaps our biggest trouble is thinking we know it all. Even when we don't disagree with the ends of marriage and the old form of the vow, we have a way of expecting the whole thing to be obvious, and to be quite capable of taking care of itself. The truth is, though, that it isn't, and doesn't; and it needs, in consequence, a lot more thought than it gets. I have a little to say about some of it in a while, but before that there are a couple of things that can make a big difference. We think in terms of images. That was true a while back on the subject of roles in marriage. It is true in bed, too. The conjugal act is performed in the presence of the remembered and unremembered pictures of sexuality that the partners have in their heads. The images are, so to speak, carved upon the posts of the marriage bed. They dominate the scene. And, as always, they may be good or they may be bad. Usually they are somewhat less than adequate, to say the least. Therefore, if there are any gilt-edged images around, we ought to be quite diligent about making as much of them as possible. I think there are such, and I am willing to name two of them. One is from the Bible, the other from literature; the Bridegroom and the Bride from the Song of Solomon, and the figure of Beatrice from Dante.

Beatrice first.

She takes us straight to the connection between the marriage bed and romantic love. Think of a crowd of people. If you are a man, imagine the women among them dressed alike and with simplicity—as peasants, for instance, or nuns. Then imagine yourself there watching, beholding. You know what will happen. For every man there will be, somewhere in that crowd, a woman who even under those conditions of concealment and plainness cannot be hid from him—who goes home hard to him. There may even be several. Without speaking, they speak easily; motionless perhaps themselves, they move him mightily. He is drawn; and drawn by a force the fair equal of any in this world. Now take the comparison out of the imagination and into history. The thing has happened, once or oftener, to every one of us. Even a picture will do it. I remember an illustration in a book I once read. It was only a line drawing of a rather thin girl standing on a hilltop with the wind in her black hair. The book has long since been forgotten, and I cannot even remember how old I was. Eight? Twelve? Not more than that. But I have been looking for that girl ever since. I suppose I have found her, too, not as such, but in hints and guesses in others.

Now why? I am not about to make much of the picture. As a matter of fact, I think I remember seeing it again years later, and being disappointed. The point is that the picture did not *cause* my wonder; rather, it spoke *to* it. I was already looking for wonder before I opened that book. What is it all about?

The cheap answer is that it's about biology—the itch. But that just won't do. First, because I have itched in lots of circumstances where I never came within a hundred miles of wonder. And second, because when I have really struck the note of wonder, I have never failed to notice that the itch was fundamentally separate from it. Sometimes it was just plain irrelevant; often, actually inimical. On the other hand, the easy, up-to-date answer is just as useless. That says that it's about conditioning—about the way my history has trained me to delight in certain key features, like dark hair or high cheekbones. But that's no answer to *why* it happens. Even if it's true, it only says *how* it works. It never even begins to answer the real question: Why is man the kind of being who responds to high cheekbones, or whatever?

To find that answer you have to get away from the biological boosters of explanations that just won't work, and the psychological knockers of things they don't understand. You have to go back to somebody who really loved and could really write: Dante. (I won't waste your time with my feeble appreciation of him—as a matter of fact, I have always found him heavy sledding. I suppose the only thing to do is learn Italian. If you want to get something really good on the subject of Beatrice, your man is Charles Williams, plus a dose of C. S. Lewis's *Allegory of Love*. Between the two of them they have gotten it down pretty well.) Dante says that romantic love is about the Mystical Body—the City—the mystery of membership in each other. Which, of course, is what I have been getting at all along. The general idea is that this astonishing thing of being lifted out of one's self by the mere sight of the beloved, this ability of the beloved to seem so much more than flesh and blood, her aptness to communicate, to come across hard, is a hint that the whole business of love was designed to be a communication. Not, mind you, the girl's communication of something *in her*, but God's communication *through her* of the mystery of the Coinherence. She is an image, a diagram, of the glory of the City—of that collection of created pieces made to tend ceaselessly toward the oneness of the Body. Admittedly that's a big order for one small girl with little more than dark hair and high cheekbones, but it happens every day, nonetheless. Not that it's often recognized as such; but it is felt to be something pretty nearly as big as that with remarkable regularity.

Of course, we usually miss the point of it all. We like to think that Beatrice is saying something about herself, and we begin, after the first wonder, to aim at her rather than the glory behind her. After the chivalry wears off, people in love usually act as if the whole process meant that they were supposed to find their fulfillment in each other—as if they were, respectively, each other's final goal. "You're the only girl in the world for me." "We were meant for each other." That, of course, is nonsense if you believe Dante. They were not meant *for* each other; they were meant to communicate the glory *to* each other. They are not gods, but ministers. Beatrice is precisely a priestly figure. She is not my destiny, but the agent, the delightful sacrament, of it. If I treat her as an end, delight is about all I can bargain for, and not even that for long. If I take her as a sacrament, I receive, along with the delight, the joy that lies behind her.

But Dante never went to bed with Beatrice. In our book, we would have to say he hardly even knew her. What, then, has Beatrice got to do with Bed?

Just this. For better or worse, we have made romance the basis for marriage. Falling in love is supposed to be the reason why people end up in matrimony. (The Church, you will recall, doesn't commit herself on the subject. Romance or family arrangement, it's all the same to her, provided they know what they're doing and are willing to stick with it till they die.) Romance as the justification for marriage is pretty much a folk invention of less than eight hundred years' standing. On the whole, it's not a bad one at all. It's mostly better than worse. For if marriage itself is the mystery written small—if it is indeed the earthly image of the union of Christ and his Church—then it would be hard to find a better starting point than the glimpsing of that same mystery in the Beloved. Dante never married Beatrice, but we feel obliged to; all in all, it is rather a good idea. As a matter of fact, the only thing wrong with it is the lies about it.

One of them I've already mentioned. It's the "You are my destiny" bit. Only God can be that, and any attempt to put so large a demand on a mere creature always comes a cropper. Besides, in marriage it's hard to keep up the appearance of being somebody's destiny; it's even hard to look like a halfway decent agent of destiny. Beatrice burning the toast, or leaving the socks unmended, is practically unrecognizable.

The other lie is just as palpable but a little trickier. "You're the only girl in the world for me" is not very often the truth. Precisely because Beatrice is only an agent of the glory, it usually turns out that the glory can be glimpsed through other agents as well. Dante spends quite a bit of time looking at other girls. There was Giovanna and there was the Lady of the Window. And for Sam Smith, there is the girl in the office or the lady next door. If he marries with the idea that the thing that has clicked with Beatrice is the one and only click he will ever have, he is usually going to be in for a surprise. Marriage is monogamous; the romantic intimation of the glory is not. It will take a bit of learning the hard way, if he is not prepared for the distinction. And if he never learns it—if he goes on believing the lies—he will do exactly what so many do:

spend his life going from one absolutely final, true and glorious love affair to the next, and believing every time that it is just as final, true and glorious. We will all most likely have a succession of Beatrices. That can be handled, and profitably. What is unmanageable is a succession of beds.

All the lies to one side, however, Beatrice does pretty well as a wife. Romantic love is about as close to the real point of marriage as anything can be: It is a mystery leading to a mystery, an absurdity inviting a further absurdity. We were meant for greatness, for glory, for the vast coinherence of the City. Our romantic notions fit that. If our marriages do not, it is not because marriage is contrary to romance, but because we have violated romance itself, have made the fatal mistake of stopping at Beatrice instead of the glory. My wife is not my destiny, and she cannot stand being treated as if she were. Romance in marriage is not the artificial prolongation of the initial wonders of courtship. I cannot be her swain ever again. But I can enter with her into the fellowship of the mystery, and that is romance indeed. Beatrice, then, lies in my bed, and grows old and worn along with me. She is the minister of more than herself; that is exactly why I need not fear for her inevitable growing less. We must decrease, but the Glory will increase. The bed is one more of the exchanges of the City.

The other image—or, better said, collection of images—is the Song of Solomon. God has, of course, taken pains with all the books of the Bible, but he was apparently extra solicitous for this one. Here the image of the coinherence, of the union of Christ and his Church, is deliberately and expressly stated in terms of marriage. The book is not only an inspired composition; the Holy Ghost has seen to it that it had the benefit of genius all the way along. First there was the author. I am utterly unable to subscribe to the view that he wrote "only a marriage poem," and that all the mystery is the work of later interpreters. Chiefly, because a great marriage poem cannot be only a marriage poem. Marriage is the sacrament of the mystery. A good description, even of "mere marriage," will perforce be itself mysterious. Besides, I think anyone capable of writing that well is quite up to deliberate and monumental *double entendre*. The second instance of genius was just as great. Somebody actually talked some kind of group into including it in the canon of Scripture. It is one of the few instances in history of a committee's getting something right. And the genius doesn't stop there. There were the geniuses who translated it into Latin and English. I would hate to have to choose between St. Jerome and the King James Bible. Both are quite beyond mere praise. And so are the geniuses among the Fathers who saw clearly the mystery in the book and wrote priceless commentaries and more poems—St. John of the Cross, for one. And last but not least, there was the modest genius who wrote the running page headings in the Authorized Version. Of course, the hatchet men have removed them from subsequent translations, but they remain in their old places, and most people still get to see them. (Just to give you an idea of the caliber of this kind of critic: In seminary, I bought a paperback series of commentaries on the Bible. They were designed for popular consumption, and written in the question-and-answer style. The section on the Song of Solomon began as follows: *Q. What book of the Bible is of even less religious value than Ecclesiastes? A. The Song of Solomon.* The rest was just as bad.)

The wonderful thing about the book, however, is that its appeal is not limited to geniuses. The peasants read it with delight. Dante is forbidding, and the commentaries on him are almost as bad as the theological obscurities I come up with. The Song of Songs is a joy. It comes across on all levels at once, and if you're not in the mood for mystery you can read it in bed and still find more than you can possibly handle. I say no more about it. Only read, mark, learn and inwardly digest it. Pray by it, or make love by it. You can't go wrong.

⁓

So much for the images around the bed. I said at the outset that it was the rosy unreality of the marriage manuals that got me down. In all honesty I have to admit that I have been getting pretty close to rosiness myself; all these high-flown images tend to have a hypnotic effect. Necessary though the principles may be, it becomes just as necessary to get back to the facts. Accordingly, the flight is now over. I touch ground on the subject of procreation.

It is the most notable end of the sexual act. It is also the most unsettled one. Ever since the development of reasonably effective contraceptive devices it has been under debate. What I have to say here is not part of my professional contribution to the discussion. It does not even begin to touch the real and pressing complexities with which the population explosion is about to visit us. It's only the personal reaction of an interested and not too innocent bystander, and it is simply this: Nobody has come up with the right answer yet. And that means nobody's church too. Everybody of course has an answer—and an answer to everybody else's answer as well—but the question *as it really is* is still waiting. Nobody is doing justice to *all* the facts. Take contraception itself for instance. The division is Roman Catholics *against*, Protestants *for*, and Episcopalians pro or con depending on whom you talk to. And it's quite a bit more complicated when you get into it. Generally, Roman Catholics are against procedures that constitute unnatural interference with conception. As a matter of fact, however, unnaturalness turns out to be rather a narrow basis on which to argue. The case it forms is consistent enough, but it is something of a moral bantamweight. After all, the biggest *moral* element in the picture would seem to be not the attendant details of execution, but the basic intention to use the sexual act in a way which will avoid having children. *That* Rome does not generally appear to consider. And for good reason. For if that intention is bad, then the rhythm system is bad: All the hairsplitting to one side, *that* is exactly the intention of couples who use the rhythm method. But if that intention is good, then the Protestant case has won the day and all we have to do is wait for the perfecting of The Pill, or the New Argument which will get us off the hook of unnaturalness. It is a vexed question.

On the other hand, modern Protestants have tended to act as if there were no moral question at all involved in the intention to use the sexual act but to avoid conception. They seem to assume that pleasure and procreation are a lot more divorcible than previous generations thought them to be. For nineteen hundred years, Christians (Protestants included) assumed that they were not divorcible at all. For nineteen hundred years, the great piece of birth-control advice handed out by all the churches was: If you don't want children, abstain. Admittedly, that's not easy; but modern Protestants act as if it were not only difficult, but somehow crazy and immoral besides. They get annoyed at Rome's hairsplitting, but they fail to see that Rome is at least trying to do justice to a principle we all shared up until seventy years ago. Remember? The Connecticut law against contraceptives was passed by a Protestant Legislature in the last century. So between Rome and Geneva, and with Anglicans landing like locusts on both sides of the fence, the situation is not too clear. The peasants can have lots of fun watching the street fight, but they get precious little practical guidance.

For myself, by the way, I am mostly for the Catholic view, and try to act and teach accordingly. The idea that nineteen hundred years of moral theology have been wrong strikes me as just plain fishy. But while I think that holding out for the non-divorcibility of intercourse and procreation is the right principle, I am not pretending I know what to do with it. Let me punch holes in my own case. On the one hand, I think the use of contraceptive devices is ridiculous, not so much on the basis of unnaturalness as on the basis of love and the dance. Between the devices and the pills, it becomes a ballet conducted via an assortment of blocks and tackle, of jibs, booms and rigging. There is just too much fuss over equipment, and too many coy but urgent little trips. On the other hand, the so-called rhythm system is not much better. While it allows the ballet to go on without all that rigging, it doesn't allow it to go on with much spontaneity. The dancers have to check with the timekeeper every time they want to go on stage. Furthermore, when he says "time" they feel obliged to dance whether they want to or not. They can get awfully tired of living under the stare of that beady-eyed calendar. And The Pill isn't going to solve any problems either. It would seem to me that anything that comes as close as the pill does to being the "moral" equivalent of a hysterectomy is going to be a pretty tricky proposition, romantically, morally and psychologically, even if it turns out to be just dandy medically. So the whole thing is a draw. Devices, pills or charts, none of it is about to improve the dance. I really think that abstinence is better than all that rigging. Seriously. I know that it sells like iceboxes to Eskimos, but sitting out a dance really can be more in the spirit of the affair than trying to lug all that armor around.

The other contests are a draw too. Rhythm is a worry: It is, in spite of claims, not effective enough to form the basis for a moral choice for the general run of people. There are just too many women with disorderly menstrual cycles. But contraception (device or pill, it matters not) is a worry too. It will never be infallible. At the very least it has to be practiced by human beings—a notoriously undependable lot. There is no contraceptive that can be made love-proof, romance-proof, martini-proof—or proof against the kind of absurd sociological whim that in the postwar years led a generation that knew all about contraceptives to produce giant families. But to the degree that contraceptives are successful, they lead people, especially women, to count more and more heavily on *not* conceiving, and, obviously, to have a growing fear of the whole chancy business. The modern wife, rhythmic or rigged, thinks of herself as playing with dynamite. Beatrice is far from her thoughts, and so is Solomon's Bride. It is not even plain pagan Venus whom she prays to in her bed. As far as she is concerned, the goddess she needs most is Lady Luck. Again, abstinence is more tolerable.

Take another instance. The feature that I like least about the modern case for contraception is the not infrequent solemnization of the sexual act. Intercourse, it is sometimes argued, is so necessary a sacrament of love that it must be made available in marriage at all costs. *Ergo,* contraception is O.K. I don't believe that. I believe intercourse is important, even big; even one of the central things. But I can't manage to take it quite that seriously. I have a sneaking suspicion that all this straight-faced piety about sexuality misses one of the Creator's most brilliant bits of humor: The body uses the same general equipment for both lovemaking and plumbing. Desire and drainage are hilariously close. I think that's a hint to take it lightly. Don't misunderstand; it should *matter,* but we shouldn't get grim about it. It is a movement of the dance, not the be-all and end-all of the dancers. Omitting it doesn't stop the show. There's nothing wrong with mutually agreed abstinence if it's honestly tried.

While on the subject of honesty, however, I hasten to admit that I don't think I can go around answering every problem by saying that abstinence would be better. That can hardly be the whole solution. Except on a temporary basis, even St. Paul wouldn't allow it. So the argument is a draw there too; I am not much different from my brothers. In every case we are quite up to taking apart the other fellow's position; we are not very good at pasting together our own. We are all hunting elephants.

One last item, not about contraception. The exaltation of the sexual act, especially by the marriage manuals, has not been terribly helpful. As I said, they get very solemn about the raptures of it all (again, don't misunderstand—I am not against raptures, only solemnity), and they work up a real mystique of intercourse, in which one of the principle magic phrases is *simultaneous orgasm.* I think it's fair to say that that's a subject most people have heard about. I even think that a lot of people have gotten the idea that it's the One Best Way of All. I think it's very odd. Admittedly, as a piece of advice to a man— namely: Be sure you try to give your wife pleasure before you take it yourself—it is excellent. Good manners are essential. There is no place where it is more fitting to be a gentleman than in bed. But. As a piece of advice to *two* people—namely: Make sure you *come* together—I find it utterly irrelevant, and dangerous too. What does one orgasm add to another? As a matter of fact what does all this thinking about orgasms add to the stature of any- body's marriage? All I think it does is to make the idea of sexual intercourse indistinguishable from the concept of mutual masturbation. And that is hardly a welcome addi- tion. The two are in fact as different as night and day. The one is self-giving, the other self-regarding; the one nat- ural, the other perverse. Perhaps I am wrong about how common this is. Maybe I have read the wrong books. All I know is that this business of synchronized desire was a big irrelevancy to me. It kept me from seeing *love* for a good long while.

I am afraid, however, that bed is not really my subject. I can see what it's about, I can criticize what's wrong, and I can more or less keep myself afloat. But that's about it. If you want something solid to hang on to, keep looking; my raft isn't going to support much weight beside my own. I think the bed matters. I am sure that if I could ever hack my way through the jungle of Sex, back to the hills of naturalness, it would matter marvelously. But even then I don't think it would be life's greatest matter. The meeting in bed is not the end. Its greatness lies in the ends that it serves. And the greatest of them all is not the meeting of a lover and beloved, or Dante and Beatrice, but the meeting of the whole Body of the Coinherence, the entrance of man into the City of God.

So the main theme returns. In bed as elsewhere, absurdity is the touchstone of our calling. The bed cannot be made foolproof, because only fools are available to occupy it, but it can be made sane. The calling is absurd, but if we will lie down with the foolishness of Christ, we can rise up with the wisdom of God. The Christian marriage Bed is strictly for sports, plungers, and heavy spenders. Double-entry bookkeepers, and sewing circle treasurers need not apply. The vow of fidelity is an absurd commitment, but it is the heart of marriage. If we will only sit still and eat our own bread till we die, we will get well. My own cure is slow in coming, but after fifteen years I think I see a few signs of strength. And that is not to be sneezed at. In this department, even to be a little better is a monumental achievement.

VI

BOARD

The geography of marriage continued; the Table analyzed and exalted; fair speech, television, canned soup, and the Liturgy of St. John Chrysostom examined and properly oriented.

THE BED MAY BE THE FIRST of the great pieces of matter in marriage, but it is by no means the only one. It is not even the most obvious: We put doors on our bedrooms, and we retire from the rest of the house when we go to them. The dining room is something else again. Whether it is a room in its own right, or a kitchen used to make shift, it is invariably central in the house. In fact, with the current fashion of open and contiguous living areas, it has, more often than not, no door at all. It is not only visible, it is unmistakable, as the sanctuary of a church is unmistakable. And in its center is the family's other great piece of matter; the Table. Duncan Phyfe or early Grand Rapids, Danish modern or discount-house chromium, the Table defines both the room it occupies and the household that gathers around it. It is the other first investment, and as long as the household lasts, it remains the one thing that everybody uses most—the one and often the only place where the family meets in fact.

Think of it first as a *thing*. To begin with, it is matter, not thought; it is not with us as the living-room furniture is with us—because we think it's a good idea; but with us as the bed is with us—because we cannot function without it. The poorest house has a table, and is by that very thing not so poor after all. But because it is a thing, because it is true to itself, it comes to us as things always come: raw, intractable and unfinished. Planks on packing crates, or polished mahogany on delicate turnings, it is only itself. It will not turn from table into Board on its own motion any more than box spring and mattress will become marriage Bed without considerable care. It is there, and it is suitable, but the household that gathers around it must work to bring it into the dance. The table enters the exchanges of the family exactly as the stage enters into the ballet: as a thing, as itself, by being faithful to its own mute and stubborn materiality. It is the floor that makes possible the marvelous leap of grace; it is also the floor that punishes the less than marvelous one with disgrace. The table can make us or break us. It has its own laws and will not change. Food and litter will lie upon it;

fair speech and venom will pour across it; it will be the scene of manners or meanness, the place of charity or the wall of division, depending. Depending on what is done with it, at it and about it. But whatever is done, however it enters, it will allow only the possible, not the ideal. No one has ever created the Board by fiat. God himself spread his table, but Judas sat down at it. There is no use thinking that all we have to do is wish for a certain style of family life, and wait for it to happen. The Board is a union of thing and persons; what it becomes depends on how the thing is dealt with by the persons.

There is one result, however, which will be produced automatically: The Board will always give birth to *liturgy*. I don't mean specifically religious liturgy here. I mean liturgy in the old sense that the word had before Christians picked it up. In that sense, liturgy is not simply a function of religion but an inevitable feature of the life of the city. The Greeks were, I think, the first to define it. In the small city-state of antiquity, each citizen was assigned a portion of the material work of the city as his personal responsibility: the repair of so many feet of wall, for example, or the construction of so many yards of drainage facility. The word they used for this assignment was *leitourgia*. They saw that community of life meant community in *things*, and that unless the citizens joined in the doing of the things, the city could not thrive. Each was to have his peculiar *liturgy*; but it was to be his as a member of the body politic, not on the basis of his private tastes. It was a brilliant notion. As cities became larger and more complex, of course, it became unwieldy. But it is precisely the absence of visible liturgy that nowadays makes the common life less obvious to common men. Twenty feet of stone wall erected at my own charges speaks clearly to me of my involvement in the city; a lever on a voting machine turned down over the name of a mayoralty candidate who will by and by appoint a commissioner of public works is a little vague. It really is the same thing, but it is not drawn as sharply—it is not so elegant a diagram. In societies that have remained small, however, in bodies which have kept their materialities simple, it still applies in its old form. The Church needs only priest, people, table, bread and wine; the union of those remains the taproot of all its liturgy. So also with the family. Parents and children, table and food are the fundamental pieces. Given these, there will develop, with absolute inevitability, a way of doing business native to that Board and its distinctive materialities. "At our house, we always have icebox cake on Daddy's birthday." That is genuine liturgy. The key to its true rationale is the phrase "We always do...." The test of its germaneness is not its conformity to some abstract standard of perfection, but simply whether it constitutes an honest doing of the work of the city with the materials at hand. Liturgy is a local matter: The Church has had almost as many liturgies as she has had altars. The massive attempts at enforced conformity to what somebody considers an ideal norm—the great master service books and universal rites—have had only middling success. And since the family is so utterly local a proposition, its truest liturgies will be home-grown—and very often peculiar, in both senses of the word. They will be wordy or brief, elaborate or plain, high or low, according to the tastes and the talents of the families that make them. But their constant feature is that they will never fail to be made. The Table is simply the kind of thing that brings them forth.

And that brings up the second point about the materiality of the table. It is not only a thing, it is a *place*. The Board is geography even more obviously than the Bed is. It is the principal territory of the family as a whole. And it is the guarantee that the household is a real society and not a legal fiction; all true societies are defined geographically. They are unities of place, not of interest; they are *bodies*, not *clubs*. The parish, the village, the city, the nation are precisely territorial entities. Principles and ideals shape them, but they do not make them. America is democratic, Russia is communistic; but they are truer to their geographical roots than to their ideal ones most of the time. America finds the Panama Canal handy for reasons that lie closer to the earth than political principle; Russia, Czarist or Communist, always looks longingly on warm-water ports. The American standard of living is due at least as much to the land and its people as to democratic ideals; the Battle of Stalingrad was a Russian victory before it was a Communist one. So too with the family. I do not associate with my wife and children because of my principles. I do it because I have to— we inhabit the same small plot of land. The soil may be rich or thin, the land peaceful or shaken by earthquakes;

we stay on because it is this or nothing. Love and fear entirely to one side, it is our land, and we are not about to move. Our roots go down around this board; all our sowing was in one bed, and all but myself have grown from the soil that is my wife. From Bed and Womb to Breast and Board, we are one by origin and by place; geography is our first unity.

The Board, then, stands as the published map of the family. The bed was our *place* of being for only minutes; the womb and the breast for no more than months; but the table is our territory literally for years. It is the great clue to the mystery of being. We have sprung from local and common roots, but we have grown into discreteness and separateness, and now we sit around this table. We do not huddle together only to keep warm or to take advantage of one another; economics and pride explain only *how* we do it, not *why*. We are no club; we meet for no purpose of our own forming. We began as pieces of a piece, common matter fragmented, but we are here because we have been invited to dance our discreteness into the mutuality of God himself. From a body we came into bodies; it is the table that now draws us into the Body that shall be. From a mother, we were born into isolation; it is the table that begins now to lift us into Jerusalem the mother of us all.

In the eighteenth chapter of the Book of Genesis, it is reported that God the Father, God the Son and God the Holy Ghost sat down once and had lunch with Abraham in the plains of Mamre. The table has been the hallmark of the Trinity ever since. The world is about the mystery by which the created order of pieces and parts is to become the image of the coinherence of the three divine Persons; about the forming of the Body of Christ, the building of the City of God. And the Board is the first of the places at which it happens. If that sounds a little fancy for your own table full of upset glasses and brawling children, remember Abraham: He set God the best table he could, but his wife embarrassed him by being rude. From his point of view, the occasion was hardly a success. As it turned out, however, it didn't matter; he became the father of the people of the coinherence anyway. The City of God began with a meal that didn't go right; your spilled milk isn't going to hold up the building of it too much.

IT WON'T HOLD IT UP, that is, if it is only spilled milk. The table has its natural intractabilities as well as its native virtues, and we can learn to work with them all. But there are other things that can come to the table that are not natural to it. There are foreign accretions and imported difficulties, and it is to those that we need to pay attention. Some of them are helpful, some not; they need sorting.

I said before that the 1950's were, matrimonially speaking, not a bad period. We did quite a bit of thinking about the family, and specifically about the table, and we brought a welter of things to it, mostly with the idea of making it work better. We rediscovered the dining room.

We revived the big family. We reinstituted the groaning board. The homemaking consultants and the food editors had a field day. They conjured up a vision of the household as a populous and bustling city, and they published reams of practical advice about how to give it flesh. In short, they trained our sights on the very thing the table was about: the movement of nature into membership. Not bad, indeed.

As usual, however, the forces of the opposition were not idle. The imports and additions to the household—the liturgies suggested to us in such profusion—did not always strengthen the table's natural aptness for building the City. The innate motion toward membership was often countered by a resident and demonic drive back in the direction of fragmentation and discreteness. For example: We discovered cooking again, and with a vengeance. The plainest house could bring off a pizza or a *coq au vin* simply by following the directions in the local supermarket family magazine. Newlyweds served Beef Stroganoff and *babas au rhum*. It was marvelous. There was a richness, an interest, on the table that had not been seen for years, if ever. Unfortunately, it was not generally followed up. No sustained effort was made to bring these liturgies of food home and make them local by adaptation. They tended to remain larks, splendid irrelevancies that found no permanent resting place. And so we missed the boat. After the novelty of the *haute cuisine* had worn off, food itself—one of the table's greatest bonds of unity—was either left pretty much as it had been, or turned into an occasion of eclectic dilettantism. Neither was any use to the family.

Again, we rediscovered wine. I firmly believe that, along with real bread, it is one of the pieces without which the Board can hardly be itself. What was even better, we put it back on the table; we drank it with our meals. But here again, the drive toward the real restoration was countered and stopped short of its goal. For most people, wine too was only a sometime thing; it never had a chance to speak its real piece in its steady and ancient voice. And for those who did put it back, the devil was ready with that most banal of all perversions, wine snobbery. What might have become a true liturgy rooted in earth and history was, with alarming frequency, reduced to a lot of high church popery-jiggery. And its advocates were, with equal frequency, crashing bores.

And then there was the dining room—and the living room and family room which were its extensions. In some resourceful designs (I am not overfond of them personally, but they were honestly liturgical) all of these areas were in sight of each other. The Board positively defined the whole; it was the true lord of the things of the household. It was in many ways the best thing we did—or, better said, the best thing we almost did, for we missed the boat there, too. We built those areas, but we made no liturgy to go on in them. As often as not, the fireplace was taken to be the center of attraction. We built conversation pits around it, and spacious living and family rooms to house it. But we produced no true liturgy by it because in this age of central heating, even a real fireplace is fake. No one really needs it; you have to go out of your way to use it. Only the real things of life can enter into liturgy. The sad part about our brilliant near miss in home design was that the great real thing—the table itself—was bypassed. As often as not, the best and truest table in the house was used only for the occasional liturgy of parties; the daily liturgies of the family had to make shift for themselves around a depressing kitchen set or at (abomination of desolation) one of those lunch-counter arrangements, fittingly called islands. We almost had the whole thing in the palm of our hand; the mainland of the table was almost conquered. But the advantage was not pressed and the initiative was lost. We continued in far too many homes to live offshore from our own territory and to wonder why we still felt homesick.

That's about where we stand now. We sit at our tables, still looking for the relevant liturgies that will restore us to our real functions and our rightful places. We are still trying to build the City, but the competition has become fierce. We are continuously being invaded by other cities: TV during dinner (let alone at other times) is precisely the overwhelming of the village by the metropolis. So is recorded music. So are frozen spinach soufflé, commercial bread and canned soup. And so are the PTA, the Rifle Club, the Boy Scouts, the Bowling League and the thousand other plausible intrusions which so disrupt the pattern of home life that no native liturgy ever forms. Don't misunderstand, however. I would not suggest for a minute that we make any attempt to turn back the clock and live without all these.

First of all, we shouldn't. They are by no means all evil. They are only other liturgies, other ways of dealing with the host of things which an abundant society showers upon us. Many, many of them are superb. The damage they cause is due chiefly to their number, to their diversity, and to their polish. There are far too many of them for anyone to use. Choice is essential; no house can possibly take everything that comes over the TV or off the supermarket shelves. More, they are far too varied: There are good programs and bad, helpful products and useless, liberating diversions and stifling ones; not only choice, but discerning choice is needed. Last, they are done with more slickness than the average home can ever manage: The music around my table does not measure up to the music in my record collection; if I use my records at the wrong time, I will smother the local liturgy of singing. And the list can go on indefinitely. The home cannot stand constant comparison with the metropolis. I know women who will not learn to cook proper rice, because precooked rice has made them ashamed of their own efforts with the genuine article. Worse, I know women who will not explore the endless and utterly local liturgy of soup, because opening cans is the only ceremony they know on the subject. What we need is discernment. Canned soups, for instance, are a brilliant device. For emergencies they are invaluable, and as an ingredient for stretching a local and peculiar masterpiece they are priceless. We just have to keep them contributory to us, to make them serve rather than dominate. We have to fight for the rights of the small town a little more zealously, and work at its liturgies a lot harder. Every man's table should develop a proud and somewhat stubborn provincialism. We don't need purblindness and mere insularity, but we are, after all, country bumpkins, and we should keep the city slickers at a respectful distance.

In the second place, we simply cannot live without the distraction and competition of the greater liturgies. We have built ourselves a way of life that makes them necessary to our existence. For example, consider our large-scale migration to the suburbs. The reasoning behind it is sound: People feel that their families will be better off as families out in the country. It is precisely in order to build the local city among themselves that they move away from the metropolis. But the move itself creates pressures and distractions. More often than not, the time spent in commutation is so great that the Board itself is broken: The father does not eat with his children. Again, the suburb is less compact than the metropolis. Most children have to go to school on buses. When they sit down to their noon meal, it is in a cafeteria; the table of their own home sees them at midday only on weekends. As a matter of fact, between disjointed breakfast schedules and fatherless suppers, the suburban household hardly meets at all on five days out of seven.

I suppose there is no immediate way around this. The system does not seem to be about to change, and we do not seem to have any practical way to get out of cooperating with it. We have to make a living. The rosy dream of packing up dolls and dishes and heading for Vermont—of settling down far out in the country—is no solution for most of us. It is, literally and figuratively, just too far out. The real solution will have to face the fact that most of us are both bound and determined to live in the kind of community we now inhabit. Monochrome though it may be, and overspecialized and distracted, too, it is the only one that will provide us with a place in which we can get the kind of money we need to pay our way, and the kind of schooling we would like to see our children have. That leaves us holding a thoroughly mixed bag.

It also defines our work. What we have to do is sort the contents of that bag, and distinguish carefully between the real items and the fake ones. The sorting will have to be precisely a sorting of *things* and, above all, of liturgies and their attendant ceremonies. As elsewhere, I have a few ideas about principles, plus a few highly local and probably untransferable adaptations to offer. They will come out by and by. Right here I want only to say something rather general.

To begin with, the job isn't easy. Partly because of all the competition I have been talking about, but partly because of the very nature of the work itself. The gluing together of a clutch of human beings into some semblance of a city has never been more than remotely possible. We are all sinners, and it's the people closest to us that see us at our worst. The family gets the lion's share of life's provocations, aggravations and enervations. Nowhere is there so much fur quite so ready to be rubbed the wrong way.

But beyond that, there is the question of the sorting itself. What precisely do I want to see around my table? There is so much, new and old, that I hardly know where to begin. I have a couple of ideas, though, and the first one is my usual pet: Try on the old hats first. Take manners, for instance. Things like sons helping their mother into her chair at dinner, like thanking her afterward, like asking to be excused from the table, like kissing people goodbye. Carry it a little farther from the table. Take not interrupting, take the rule that one person talks at a time, take knocking on doors before bursting into a room, take "How do you do," and "Please," and "Thank you." They are all very old-hat, but who will say they're not becoming? No advances in technology preclude them, no alterations in manner of life have made them fake; they are rooted in the nature of man and the exchanges of the city. But if you take them, remember one thing. They are not ideas, they are liturgies; they are only good when they become simply *the way we do things*, when they acquire the naturalness of an old priest making the sign of the cross. That puts a very large burden on parents. First, they will have to have enough sensible manners of their own to make the drive convincing; and second, they will need perseverance. It is very, very hard. It takes years. And maybe 80 percent of it will inevitabley be waste motion. Decent liturgies don't come easily; even if they are not driven out by positively demonic ones, a lot of perfectly good ritual simply falls by the wayside because nobody was quite prepared for the heroic labor of keeping it going.

Manners are only an example. There are dozens of other old hats. There are parties—the liturgical celebrations of the city's history. There are vacations: the city's forays into other lands for conquest and plunder, and for memories of derring-do to be recounted down the years after coffee and dessert. There are hobbies: the city's exaltation of the peculiar talents of its singers, its painters, and its whittlers. All of these liturgies are as old as man; they will never cease to be contemporary. On the Day of Judgment someone will be taken in the act of rigging a ship model; another will be left while blowing out the candles on his birthday cake. We are not quite as far at sea as we think we are. The ancient rites of the home are as good as new, if we work at them.

What about the new hats, though? Well, here is where the sorting comes in full force. Think of television. I think I was one of the last holdouts against it. I still think it is a dangerous monster. But the assassination of the President convinced me that it was a monster whose cage I had to enter. I may tame it, or it may eat me, but I must face it. The great city has become so great that television is a necessity. It is precisely our marketplace, the one center where we can all meet and talk and look. All of us watched the caisson move down Pennsylvania Avenue; we all saw our own faces file past his coffin in the Rotunda. For a society of such unintelligible complexity, it was a fabulous achievement. Of course, as a true marketplace, TV is also filled with trash, hucksters and shoddy merchandise. My small city needs only enough of that to teach it to be healthily suspicious of strangers, and of Greeks bearing gifts. Therefore, the liturgy of watching television needs constant revision and refinement. But note that it is precisely a liturgy. If my children watch *Huckleberry Hound* for three weeks running, no one can talk them out of the fourth: "We *always* watch *Huckleberry Hound* on Thursdays." *We do*, you see; the liturgy of St. John Chrysostom has neither more nor less justification than that. But with anything that powerful, the work of taming it isn't going to be easy. My television, for example, may not be turned on during dinner; the great city will overwhelm my little village. I have few local liturgies capable of winning out over Huntley, Brinkley and *The Three Stooges*. Even *The Mickey Mouse Club* is frequently too much for us. Again it should not be allowed so to monopolize time that hobbies, reading and schoolwork have to operate on its leavings. This is all obvious, but it all happens. It needs endless and forceful watching.

And television is only one example. There are records—the liturgy of listening: I must watch that it doesn't destroy the local liturgy of singing, playing, and telling my own stories. When I go to a man's house, I should hear *his* children, not the Kingston trio; *his* jokes, not Shelley Berman's. And there are outside activities— the broadening liturgies by which the family becomes the beneficiary of its members' involvement in Power

Squadron or Integration Movement: Watch that they don't so disrupt the domestic liturgy that there is no time to share the benefits.

But enough. We need good liturgies, and we need natural ones; we need a life neither patternless nor over-patterned, if the city is to be built. And I think the root of it all is *caring*. Not that that will turn the trick all by itself, but that we can produce nothing good without it. True liturgies take things for what they really are, and offer them up in loving delight. Adam naming the animals is instituting the first of all the liturgies: speech, by which man the priest of creation picks up each of the world's pieces and by his wonder bears it into the dance. "By George," he says, "there's an *elephant* in my garden; isn't that *something*!" Adam has been at work a long time; civilization is the fruit of his priestly labors. Culture is the liturgy of nature as it is offered up by man. But culture can come only from caring enough about things to want them really to be themselves—to want the poem to scan perfectly, the song to be genuinely melodic, the basketball actually to drop through the middle of the hoop, the edge of the board to be utterly straight, the pastry to be really flaky. Few of us have very many great things to care about, but we all have plenty of small ones; and that's enough for the dance. It is precisely through the things we put on the table, and the liturgies we form around it, that the city is built; *caring* is more than half the work.

VII

THINGS

Materialism vindicated; but the shortage of honest matter viewed with alarm. The author warms to his subject and presents himself as an incurable hobbyist. Readers put off by such self-display are tempted back with offerings of strudel and vintage wine.

I T IS SOMETIMES EASY to get the impression that Christians take a dim view of *things*—that they are much more in favor of indifference than caring. There is a lot of clucking over the evils of what is referred to as this materialistic age, and most people just take it at face value. But we are not a materialistic age at all. We would be better off if we were. We are the most devil-ishly spiritual of all ages: Poor old matter, like poor old flesh, takes a bad drubbing. Far from caring too much for it, we are forever busy beating it out of its natural shape into fetishes and status symbols which are more to our liking. Matter itself gets very few chances to speak. And therefore the usual sermons against it are off base. It isn't matter that's opposed to spirit—the two were designed to go together; what is opposed to spirit is perverted matter, uncared-for matter, unloved and unlovely matter. And matter doesn't get that way on its own steam. It is perverted precisely by being cared for irrelevantly by spirit, by being loved, not for what it *is*, but for what it does for me and means to me.

True enough, Christians are told to deny themselves material things, but it's very easy to miss the point. The goal of all Christian self-denial is the restoration, not the destruction, of nature; the removal, not of matter, but of perversion. The saint fasts in order that someday his body, with all its parts and desires, may become whole and operative again. He is emphatically not trying to cease caring about matter. He is not in the business of stripping off a useless cocoon in order that the beautiful butterfly of his real self can fly free. The Christian religion is not about the soul; it is about man, body and all, and about the world of things *with* which he was created, and *in* which he is redeemed. Don't knock materiality. God invented it.

Matter is actually more of a help than a hindrance to spirit. A soul without a body is a ghost; the traditional notion of ghosts as poor, lonely, helpless beings is sound. Without my body I am only half a man. Nor does Christ himself seem to spend much time complaining about materiality. He seems, in fact, to have enjoyed it. His reputation as a glutton and winebibber, undeserved though it undoubtedly was, must have had some foundation in fact. He seemed to *care* and he seems to intend that we should care, too. It's not only that our lives inevitably will be involved with matter, but that they ought to be. Adam is made in the image of God. If God made things because he liked them, God's image should not be surprised to find that, in his own proportion, he likes them too. Adam is the priest of creation. His truest work is to offer up reality itself, not just a headful of abstractions about it. Only the perversions of matter can be wrong. Things, as such, are never bad; they are not even indifferent. They are positively good. Let a man just once really face fish or fowl, bread or wine, shoelace or gummed label, and he will know he has by no means lowered himself. In lifting them up, he himself grows taller.

What we need to work up is a Christian materialism, and nowhere do we need it more than in the home. Marriage and family life are practically an inundation in matter. The world of the household is one long continuum of things; bed and board, food and drink, runny nose and soggy diaper are inescapably with us. Not all of them require the same degree of caring, but they all deserve a fair share, and we very commonly give it. With each man, however, the caring will be unique and personal. I cannot tell you what to care about. All I can manage to give you along these lines is a list of the things *I* care about, and a few peculiar reflections as to why. The only general remarks possible seem to be centered on the nature of caring, its marks and manifestations.

Take the marks first. I think *possessions* are the chief evidence of caring. Not that there aren't many things we could all care about if we had the time or the money to afford them. There are, and as we acquire time or money, we should keep our eyes peeled for them. It is sad to see a man enter a more prosperous and leisured condition with the intention only to care more industriously about what he already likes. My wife says that as a child she cared mightily about condensed milk. So, I think, did my aunt: so much so that they both looked forward to adulthood and independent income as the occasion for the eventual possession and enjoyment of an unrestricted number of cans of condensed milk. Mercifully for us all, neither of them ever tried to realize the hope. They grew, and their caring grew with them. But though it grew, it grew only within the realm of the possible; even their expanded caring has not yet managed to attain to chinchilla and Cadillac. Time and money restrict us all.

But within those limits, possessions really do become the prime evidence of what we care about. The woman I delight in becomes *my* wife. The man I care about becomes *my* friend. The food I like becomes *my* dinner; favorite china, *my* china; a desired guitar, *my* guitar. All, to be sure, in so far as possible: but save for that limitation, if I care, I seek to possess. I do, and I should. Covetousness, greed, the lust for ownership, is only—is precisely—the perversion of care. It is the love not of things or people, but of *having*. It makes a good, not of goods, but of *gain*; and, in the long run, it makes a man quite unable to care for the real goods at all.

Two things follow from this. First, if care is shallow, possessions will be discarded. (They slip away, too, and they wear out, but that isn't our doing.) The man who buys a boat will soon enough find out whether boating is one of his real cares. Our possessions make demands upon us; they form us as much as we form them. Most of us have an attic or a basement in which we bury the remains of our former fascinations. We once felt deeply about photography or golf, but over the years we learned differently. Closet and dump now hide the corpses of our shallow cares. With mere things, of course, the learning process is quite painless; all we lose is some time, a little money and perhaps a small quantity of face. But when it is our care for people that proves to have been trifling, the results are usually tragic. The discarded home-movie outfit is one thing, the discarded wife or child quite another. In either case, however, possession proves or disproves care.

Second, things are true to themselves, and must be loved for themselves. I begin my approach to everything and everybody as if it or he were my own bright idea. More, I most often buy on the same basis. But as the years wear down, I find there is more to it. I may begin with a notion in my head, but what I actually come to possess is both more and less than my bright idea: I get a thing or a person whose first concern is not *my* care but *its* own being. I get something which will prove my care on the stumbling block of its own stubborn materiality. You can buy a recorder, because you look on it as a flattering unction: It says something about your status as the modern version of Renaissance man. But you will stay with the recorder only if you really care for the recorder. The thing itself is limited, minor, and quite intractable. You will have to love it for itself if you are to put up with its nonsense. Status is never enough of a reason for possession. Things demand more of us than we think. They are not waiting around simply to add a grace note to our mental symphony of being. They insist upon being met in person, on being loved. If they are not, they will sooner or later insist upon being left.

Perhaps the largest single trouble with our abundance of possessions is the fact that so many of them are owned, not because of what they are, but because of what they confer on us. They are there, but we seldom look at *them*. We have so much, but we love precious little of it for itself. After the itch of the mind has been scratched, matter itself goes into the discard; the junkyard is the true monument of our society. We have the most marvelous garbage the world has ever produced. Literally. Have you ever looked hard at a tin can? Don't. It will break your heart to throw it out, all silver and round and handy. But the truth is you have to throw it out. We produce so much that there isn't time or room to keep it. What is sad, though, is that the knack of wonder goes into the trash can with it. The tinfoil collectors and the fancy ribbon savers may be absurd, but they're not crazy. They are the ones who still retain the capacity for wonder that is the root of caring. When a little boy finds an old electric motor on a junk heap, he is pierced to the heart by the weight, the windings, and the silent turning of it. When he gets it home, his mother tells him to throw it out. Most likely he will cry. It is his first and truest reaction to the affluent society. He usually forgets it, but we shouldn't. He is sane; society isn't. He possesses because he *cares*. We don't.

The little boy won't carry us all the way, however. Finding wonders in the rubbish isn't enough; we show our care as much by the size of our effort as by the fact of possession. It is not only whether we have, but how hard we work at having, at holding, and at using, that is the test of care. I look around at my library. It looks like a priest's library, all right, but it says one thing very loudly to anyone with enough background to catch it: This priest is not a scholar. He thought he was one once, and began to act like one once, but his library proves that real scholarship is not his real care. There are too many holes in the crucial sections, and too much filler even where there aren't holes. This is a day laborer's library: real care in a few spots, but no monumental absorption across the board. I look at my collection of recorders. That says something different. Here is somebody who really cares. Time and effort have been put in on this. There is a real progress toward the best. I look at my wine cellar. It is small, but it says even more complimentary things than my recorder collection.

Now, the fascinating thing about my odd assortment

of cares is that each care stands on its own feet. Its first justification is not its importance but its depth. I care a lot about wines and music; but I am better at theology and Greek than at either of my apparently more careful cares. That is due to talent. It is the old story of the professional baseball player working hardest at his golf game. It is the way we are built, and while it can get badly out of hand, it is not all bad. The real point remains: *Caring* is what counts most. Any effort spent in caring for even a minor good is on the side of the angels. And it is contagious; the minor can spread to the major. I developed a time schedule for writing only after I successfully made time to practice the recorder. I acquired a working knowledge of what care *felt* like, and then transferred it to a field where I knew I should care more than I did.

Now, it is precisely the ignorance of what care feels like that is one of the roots of our trouble. We are unprepared for effort; it has become far too easy to achieve the results of care without caring. If I have to travel to the theater, my care is reinforced—I have a stake in the venture. If all I have to do is throw a switch in my living room, my care grows weaker. The process is not of course inevitable, but it is frighteningly common. Boys will not learn to care for the crafts because the minimal effort involved in assembling the usual plastic kit leads them to shy away from the real operations. It leaves them unprepared for the long labor of learning to plane edges straight by hand or turn a bead properly with a skew chisel. And it isn't just boys. All of us can achieve overnight, via one bright idea and the installment plan, things for which we would otherwise have made much longer and larger efforts, and which we would have loved more in the end. My mother painted her own china by hand over the course of many years. Quite apart from its superb good taste, it is a testament of care. In my boyhood, it drove me mad to have to be so fussy with it, but I am glad now I grew up with it. I take great pains to bore my children with the details of its origin. They should know what care can do. Neither they nor I need very many of the ready-to-run gadgets or easy-to-build kits the world offers us. Not that the kits themselves are bad—for those who have already learned to care, they are marvelous examples of the loving devotion of planners and die makers. It's just that they tend to reinforce the carelessness all around us. The society is moving toward the dangerous situation in which only a few will be able to care enough to bother about excellence. At that point we will be sitting ducks for anybody's hunt.

The final thing I would call a mark of care is the absence of big mistakes. This is more relative than the others, to be sure—real accidents do happen and some people are accident-prone—but it is still worth mentioning. We like to think that our big trouble is weakness of will; we act as if we really had a hard time bringing anything off. But that's not true. The things we really care about in a big way get done with remarkable efficiency. If we continually fail to bring off something we think we care about, it may well be that we don't really care as much about it as we thought we did. I'm not going to press this; talent has a lot to do with success, and so, to a degree, does plain unvarnished luck. But all that to one side, effectiveness is a good test of caring. My mother, after all, did finish her china. I, after all, do know quite a bit about wines and recorders. My wife, after all, can bring off a six-course dinner. The real point is not that there aren't things that can wreck even the most careful caring, but that there are points in every subject beyond which you can't go without care. It is at those places that the careless man makes his big mistake and blows the whole thing.

This is true in everything, but it is especially true when it comes to dealing with what is most important of all: people. We take up with other people for all kinds of reasons. If we really care for *them*, there will very likely be no big mistakes; but if we care mostly for what they mean to us or do for us, we can, and usually will, make some whoppers. Most divorces and wrecked friendships are the result of care that was just too small to prevent the big blunder. At the outset, it seemed big enough for anybody, no doubt, but time is the real test. This isn't quite as dire as it sounds. First of all, care does tend to repair mistakes; therefore any care, even inadequate, may help as long as it is not deliberately killed off. Second, care can be learned; it can be deepened by acting as if you had it, by doing the things that constitute the true marks of care, even if you have to do them a bit woodenly at first. There is a place for pretense, as long as the basic intention is not to fool the onlookers, but simply to care more.

Now at this point, you may have noticed something. Most of my illustrations of caring have so far come from the realm of hobbies. Let me defend the choice. It seems to me that in the kind of society we now have, and in the even more automated, canned and quick-frozen one into which we are headed, hobbies will inevitably constitute the most intelligible areas of caring open to the likes of us. One qualifier. If a man can find work that really consumes him—if he can care so greatly for his job that in every waking hour he burns over his real work— then what I am saying about hobbies applies to him in his work. Such men and women are rare. They are either great producers or great crackpots, but they are single-minded and single-cared as the rest of us are not. St. Augustine does not seem to have had a hobby; Bach's side interest seems to have been just more music. There is nothing quite like that kind of care, but it depends on two things not available to the general membership of the crowd: considerable talent and really fascinating work. Talent has, of course, always been in short supply; but in our day fascinating work is also getting harder to come by. As the machines become more refined, it begins to look as if only the machine designers will have anything genuine to care about. The rest of us will just be babysitters for their brain children. Of course, there is always the hope that automation could be made to fulfill its promise, and actually do all the routine work, and that, at the same time, creative and absorbing jobs could be provided so that we could all have work worthy of care. It's a hope, all right, but don't hold your breath. In the meantime, it would be better to pursue some more likely minor cares as hobbies.

Furthermore, even people with fascinating jobs have hobbies. The world is indeed full of a number of things. It not only invites the interest of the open-eyed; it practically extorts it. The guitar, for example, is a world in itself; even a partial exploration is utterly captivating. So, I suppose, is skiing for the sportsman, boats for the yachtsman, and cooking for the true amateur. And there is the word. The amateur. The lover who sees that play matters. When God made the world it is unlikely that he found it hard work. All the pictures of drudges slaving over watchmaking are not nearly as good a likeness of the Creator as one little boy blowing soap bubbles through his thumb and forefinger. He doesn't do it because he has to—only because he likes to. The magnificent result is not labored but thrown off in an odd moment. A true hobby is the achievement through play of something very close to the creator's own delight.

Unfortunately, we frequently misunderstand. We tend to look on a hobby as a diversion; what it really is is a concentration. Anybody who has had a real hobby knows that it is always potentially a tyrant. It can ruin your sleep, empty your wallet and monopolize your time. It needs watching, but nonetheless it is about as close to the truth of things as most of us ever get. The model locomotive builder at his basement bench is a priestly recluse. The ski enthusiast practicing alone on the slope is a true hermit of the natural religion of things. Man is set apart in order to offer and to worship. The hobbyist sees his vocation precisely as a personal call to do it himself.

Do it yourself. The phrase is solid. It is a testimonial to the fact that no matter how far gone the age may be, nature still fights back. Even the coming great automated beehive finds itself incongruously (but mercifully) encouraging hobbyists. Nature fights. But it has a long way to go to win. The sad thing about so many of the hobbies that are available is that they are tackled only with the modest enthusiasm appropriate to diversions. And worse than that, a lot of the stuff offered to us for our care is just plain fake. I look at my sons' plastic kits. The box advertises: embossed details. What a monumental giveaway of the whole phony system by which we are taught to care chiefly for results rather than things. Details grow out of care; they cannot be embossed. I remember making model furniture as a teenager. One piece was a colonial drop-leaf table. I had to make the hinges by hand—four of them, ¼" x ¼", out of sheet tin and pins. It took hours and it took care, but it was a triumph that no plastic snap hinge with embossed screws and fake joints can ever match. Some years back I made a 50-inch model sailboat controlled by clockwork and steered by a home-made version of what is known as a Fisher vane gear. I made all my own hardware and mechanism. The whole thing was exactly a priestly experience. I am a priest, and I know how close the two are. Detail is the hallmark of care; embossing is the triumph of result. And we live in an embossed society. The paper napkins are embossed, the plastic kits are embossed, and most of the rest of the paraphernalia comes out of molds. Dolls and toys, bottles and boxes, have only the shape we arbitrarily stamp upon them. The matter itself goes begging. Listen.

It is possible to buy a plastic guitar, designed for children, and equipped with a gadget that clamps over the fingerboard. It is very clever. Out of the top of it project buttons on which are embossed the names of various chords, G, C, D^7, and so on. The buttons are connected to bars which press down the appropriate strings at the proper frets. The sales pitch is: Even a child can play the guitar. People think it's great. I think it is dreadful. It's fake all the way through. It has nothing more to do with guitar playing than pressing a jukebox button does. It is aimed not at the marvelous materiality of the guitar, but at the production of a distinctly inferior result. It is strictly an embossed detail, music slapped on from the outside. And there is so much else like it that it makes your blood run cold. I'll skip over the cake mixes and the frozen sauces and proceed directly to the last abomination: canned Chinese food. Of all the master strokes by which man has really paid attention to the matter he deals with, Chinese cooking may well be the most brilliant. No vegetables receive more appropriate and loving care; in no other case are they cooked more quickly or served more freshly colored and flavored. How can a society in its right mind even conceive of equating the real thing with a canful of soggy celery, limp onions and waterlogged Oriental goodies? I will tell you how. By first of all ignoring the real merits of the thing itself, and then selecting one aspect of it for makeshift imitation. They throw in some garlic and ginger, and suggest that you drown the whole mess in domestic soy sauce, which again is about as much like the genuine article as salted shellac.

No care for things. Therefore no love of detail. Therefore more and more embossed fakes. And therefore, no excellence. And of all the societies that can't afford this kind of nonsense we are absolutely it. We are so highly elaborated, so completely wired and mechanized, that the failure of even one soldered connection could mean the loss of the whole world. Yet except for a few specialists, we are producing a race less and less likely to bother about anything. We are simultaneously expanding detail and shrinking care. Our comeuppance may well make no long tarrying.

Now, all this comes *home* with a vengeance. It isn't only a matter of embossed doilies and canned chow mein. Half the things around us aren't real. The average house is filled with fakes: fake drawer pulls and fake drawers, cast-iron trivets made of plastic, and table lamps made out of fake coffee grinders, fake pastry and fake whipped cream, cheese spread full of vegetable gum, and not even an old jar of unhydrogenated peanut butter to take the curse off it all. We are being dealt with at removes. And we are beginning to deal at removes. We are so used to getting the fast result that we have no patience for detail. Care does not come in a pressurized can; accordingly, it is not our kind of item. We have developed some of the worst features of what used to be referred to as the idle rich. We use, but we use without attention and without appreciation. We sometimes have a general notion of what is excellent, but we can't manage the detail required to reproduce it. We just don't care enough to bother.

Item. My wife makes Danish pastry. The real thing—all butter and homemade almond filling. When people taste it they know right away it's good, though most of them really don't know how good. Nevertheless, in any group there are usually one or two who say, "This is delicious; you must give me the recipe." When they hear it, their jaws drop. They simply cannot conceive of even beginning to care enough to master the pastry technique which is essential to good Danish. And even if they did, 90 per cent of them would still ask the other eternal question: "Can you substitute margarine for the butter?" They love results, but they are unprepared for the fuss required to produce great ones.

Item. Every now and then my wife and I pitch in and make strudel, usually in the fall when the apples are perfect. The result is first-class; people rave. As usual, though, the girl who wants the recipe is right in there pitching. When it is finally explained to her, we get even blanker looks than before. Danish is fussy, but strudel is practically nothing but baked detail. I tell them patiently about slamming the dough on the pastry board a hundred times, about letting it relax in a warm place for half an hour, about flouring a whole tablecloth, about rolling the dough, and about removing finger rings and wristwatches before you begin the crucial work of stretching it with the backs of your hands till it covers the dining room table. That's only the beginning, of course, but most of them fall away before that much is over. As far as they're concerned, it's just too High Church. They are totally unprepared for the fact that it is precisely all that detail that makes the difference. Every bit of it was designed out of respect for the matter in hand. There isn't an idle ceremony in the whole rite.

Item. When I serve a really good bottle of wine, I am fussy. I don't have very many of the *grands seigneurs*, but I do manage to keep a few of their near neighbors in the more reasonable price ranges. I would not think of uncorking my Cos d'Estournel '45 or my Lynch-Bages '52 or my Corton-Charlemagne '59 at the last minute before serving. The cork must come out an hour or so in advance, to let the air go to work on the bouquet. I explain this to anybody who makes the mistake of seeming interested. He looks at me as if I were some kind of pretentious snob with a penchant for baroque rituals. "Come, now," he says, "it doesn't make that much difference. I always uncork mine just before serving, and it tastes very good." I usually mumble something polite and non-directive at him, but someday I'm going to say what I think: O.K., friend, have it your way, but don't tell me there's no difference. If you can't tell good from great, so much the worse for your taste buds; I can, and it's loving detail that separates them.

That's enough. I could go on endlessly about the

whole culture without even leaving the table. In one short phrase: We are being flooded with matter about which nobody gives a damn. But the really frightening part is that the attitude begins to rub off. No home can be built without that love of detail which is the hallmark of care, yet we seem to be getting less and less able to bother. People cannot be fed without detail, children cannot be taught manners without detail, wives cannot be kept happy without detail. But in our superspirituality, we expect that a handful of good intentions and a headful of bright ideas are quite enough to make a home. The truth is, though, that matter will break us unless we love it for itself and start paying some very careful attention to its demands. We are not angels; there are no disembodied intelligences in my household. We are all *things* here, from the raisins in the cake to the father at his table. For the likes of us there is no middle ground between care and catastrophe.

VIII

ROOTS

Having bribed the reader into staying with him, the author proceeds once more to abuse their relationship, this time by introducing his relatives and an even wilder assortment of cares.

B ILLY, YOU ARE A PATIENT MAN INDEED, sitting out here and listening to an American imitation of a slightly stoned Irish pub orator discoursing on morality. It's not every man who has the charity and good manners to put up with a theological Brendan Behan. But since I am just beginning to warm to my subject, I shall presume upon your patience and become more personal still. I shall tell you where I think my own peculiar caring came from.

I grew up as an only child, but the lot fell to me in a fair ground. Let us now praise famous men, and our fathers that begat us. I begin with my grandfather, the family's patriarch of care. My father's father was an Englishman. In his younger days he worked as a butler in various households, though during the depression and up to retirement he fell in with a catering outfit. He lived next door. We were all broke during the thirties, but he was the poor man's rich man of the neighborhood. He always had candy, he always gave out pennies, and he was, accordingly, always followed by children. His pockets were gold mines. He would come home from a job with the most fantastic assortment of things: fancy string, Jordan almonds, and menus. And for the more discerning he could usually turn up something elegant: I ate more caviar between the ages of six and nine than I have ever even looked at since. Our main dishes may have been badly stretched, but the anteprandial was done in the grand style. And there were cheeses, and really good butter, and now and then an odd bottle or two tucked in the tail of his coat. (In moral theology this whole business comes under the somewhat forbidding title of *occult compensation*. Let the moralists fight it out. All I know is that he took only to give away. He was the most generous man I ever met. As far as I can recall, he never seemed to have, or want, anything for himself. The word *mine* was hardly in his vocabulary.)

And that's only the beginning. He was funny, a real clown. My grandmother was a great woman, but her most obvious characteristics were those of a tough Swede. She was a professional cook, and a good one, and a born manager besides. She took a uniformly no-nonsense approach to life. My grandfather never fought with her, but he won most of the time. He was a master of the indirect approach, the well-timed feint, and the opportune deaf ear. She could have driven any other man straight up the nearest wall, but his household was sweetness and light. And so was his life. He was devout. For a great many years he was the only churchgoer in the family. I was sent, but he went. No comments, no lectures; he just went, week after week, year after year, for as long as I can remember. And he was gracious everywhere. He was always dressed and polished. He was a genial host. He did beautifully, and without comment, what the rest of us have to make a big deal of. In one word, he cared. He cared about everything and everybody. He had the widest-open eyes of any man I have ever known.

He had, for example, a *thing* about lead foil. He owned a ball of it the size of a grapefruit. And it was the genuine article too—the kind that Salada tea used to come in. I can still recall the smell, and the wonder of its weight. But his most notable cares were baseball and fishing. I remember whole days with him, standing on the Crossbay Boulevard bridge trying to lift a few crabs or flounders out of Jamaica Bay. He was the original gentleman peasant. There we were, just two beads in the great string of city dwellers leaning over the parapet with our lines and traps, but we kept the lunch hour with solemnity. We anticipated its arrival, began it with ceremony and relished it at leisure. I remember the Polo Grounds too.

The man across the street had something to do with the private police at the place and anybody on our block was welcome to free admission. I hated baseball, but I went anyway because my grandfather loved it, and it was fun to go with him. I never quite saw the point of his absorption until I grew up. He would make a hand-ruled score card—the kind you can buy ready-printed now—and he kept a careful statistical record of the game as it proceeded. You see, he loved the thing itself. I don't hate baseball any more and I understand my grandfather a little better. Baseball is the statistical sport. Every ball thrown, every bat swung, becomes a matter of record, a piece of history. The true baseball fan does not simply watch the game; he keeps the whole city of baseball. For him, the man at bat stands in the presence of Ty Cobb, the pitcher on the mound plays under the judgment of Christy Mathewson. My grandfather really loved what was there to be loved. Not the occasional one-to-a-game sensation, but the whole solid tissue of the great American sport. When he grew old and ill, my father made him a radio set and he went on loving baseball as long as he could listen to anything. The score cards and the statistics were right there with him. (The set, by the way, had to be equipped with earphones, because my grandmother wouldn't stand for all that racket. He was a true fan though: I don't think he ever even considered the thing an obstacle. He lived just long enough to see the beginnings of television. Too bad. He was one man who could have used it to perfection.)

I do not expect to see the likes of him again. My

father was, and I am, very different from him. Somewhere along the line, maybe from the irascible Swedish stock, we picked up quick tempers. But different though we were by disposition, we got more from him than anyone else. We learned to care, perhaps in our own short-fused way, but learn we did. As far as I can recall, my father never went near a baseball game he could possibly avoid. He certainly never fished. But what a wealth of loves he had. He could draw, and he did. And well. He could paint and etch. He could sing, and he played a good banjo and an impressive mandolin. He went into photography up to his eyebrows. I have never even touched the subject, but I remember standing in his darkroom under the dim red light and watching pictures appear out of nowhere in the developer. He built radios, and gadgets and home-made inventions; and all this before the days of precut parts and preassembled kits. He died too soon too; he didn't make retirement. He never had a leisurely chance to implement his first-class caring with some of the great tools and materials the current age has come up with. He again was one who could have discerned between the real and the fake.

My own cares are very largely like my father's— mechanical, musical, and manual—but I don't think there is a single really common item in the list. It's only the caring itself that came through loud and clear. I can't draw or paint worth beans. Electricity has never inter- ested me in the least. Unlike him, I am a modelmaker at heart—a very peculiar beast indeed, as only another

modelmaker will know. I am a musician of sorts too, but
not my father's sort. I was much too high-brow for him,
what with my recorders and my harpsichord and all. We
did get together before the end though. I gave him a new
mandolin after I had taken up the guitar, and one day
we all sat down, my mother at the harpsichord, and my
father and I plucking and picking for all we were worth.
It made a rather tinkly sound, but it was a coincidence of
caring, and that's nothing to sneeze at.

And then there is my mother. If *de mortuis nil nisi
bonum*, how much more so, *de vivis?* She is still very much
with us. She formed my mind, and hammered what manners I have into shape. By anybody's standard she was a
meticulous housekeeper. You hate that sort of thing when
you are young, and I suppose even now I tend to steer
clear of it, but it's not a bad thing to grow up with. At
least you learn how to handle things that matter. But she
could be light too. She had a real flair for dialect jokes,
and could imitate almost anybody. I seem to recall days
on end when we could carry on all our conversations in an
Irish brogue or a Low Dutch accent. Her own mother was
Scotch, and very old even when I knew her. My mother's
Scotch imitations were among her best. And she recited
poetry—sometimes in German. The *Erlkönig* was one
of her repertory performances, as was also a piece that
began: "Ahem. My name is Norval; and on yon Grampian
hills my father feeds his flock." I still don't know where it
came from, but I learned to love language from that sort
of thing.

During the depression, both my parents had to work. My father worked for the New York City Park Department, and at one time lettered signs for Barnard College. (In the palmy days, he had been in business for himself as a decorator. He designed the interiors for some New York houses, and even did the décor on a couple of yachts—I think Mellon's *Avalon* was one.) My mother sold furniture at Ludwig Baumann's. The evening meal brought out the raconteur in her. She was in lamps, tables and occasional pieces, and for supper we got the day's highlights, complete with dialect, usually Jewish. She cared about words—and seriously enough to play with them. But she made them matter too. The dictionary usually came on with dessert; anything vague or unknown was looked up. I only hope I do as well by my own children.

But last of all there is my wife. Not that she is exactly one of my roots. She is more like a tree in whose beneficent shadow I am fed and watered. To be sure, some of her present cares are ones I foisted upon her to start with—she wasn't a cook at all before we married. But now. Words fail. She is abundance itself, and competence in the bargain. She can, as I said, bring off a six-course masterpiece with no more help than her husband and older children, if that's help. She knows wines and food, and she can put on the best without putting on the dog. But it is her ordinary cooking that is really spectacular. Soups. Except for a few set pieces like Vichyssoise or a Swedish repertory item called Emperor Soup (fancy beef stock, plus Madeira, plus cream, plus egg yolks), they are never the same twice. They are always *ad hoc* and almost always *ad gloriam*. Pasta. But with sauces that shout with flavor, and with fillings that cannot lift their heads for weight of cheese and meat. Chinese cooking. She picked it up one Lent and has worked at it over the years. She can now fill eight people and put smiles on their faces with rice, three pork chops and a huge panful of beautiful vegetables. Bread. Plain bread, cheese bread, raisin bread, soda bread, saffron bread, limpa, stollen and panettone; brioches, savarins, rolls, croissants; cream horns, galettes, napoleons and Danish. Specialties. Tripe Niçoise, my all-time favorite; bluefish, our greatest local delicacy, supplied all summer by fishing parishioners, and cooked a dozen different ways, the most impressive being a whole six-pounder baked with mushroom stuffing and shrimp sauce; shrimp with wild rice, mixed with the sauce from Fanny Farmer's Breslin baked bluefish and done in individual au gratin dishes. And the best part of all is that she gets better all the time. She has of course her blind spots. She has never made a decent cake in her life. Or a decent icing. She can't even get a packaged mix to work right. But I am happy with what I've got. To be sure, I put my two cents in rather frequently, and I do go around dreaming up new departures for her, but I can't take too much credit for the results. Her own love of what she is doing is the real source of it all; it would never have grown the way it has just because of my care.

Needless to say, my wife has other virtues. She has card sense, she has horse sense, and she is marvelously easy to get along with. And she puts up with me, which will probably get her a whole constellation of stars in her crown. But as I said, words fail. I make an abrupt halt right here.

Anyway I think the point is made. I grew up with people who cared, and I live with people who care; the specific items don't rub off too often, but the *caring* does. With a little luck, maybe the recipe will work again, and we will produce a few members of the next generation who will be able to bother enough to love. Right now I'll give you just one instance of the dividends of it all.

As you see, I am partial to the fruit of the vine. All my family were and are. I have made more of it than any of them but there are literally generations of care behind me. When I was growing up, table wine was the mark of a festive occasion. My father's tastes were more American than mine. He preferred cocktails and tall drinks; sparkling Burgundy was about his maximum speed in wines. Nevertheless there was, even in the hardest times, usually something to drink before dinner, and I cannot remember a time when I was not allowed a sip appropriate to my age. There were also cordials afterward. Swedish *Punsch* remains for me the true link with the great meals in my father's house. The result was that I learned to care, but to care in an ordinary way. I never saw wine or spirit used for any other end than the enjoyment of wine or spirit. I never saw my father or my grandfather drunk—and to the best of my knowledge, they never were. (The whole family, admittedly, had a wondrous capacity: The amount of stuff on which they never got drunk was quite amazing.)

For myself, I have worked for years at collecting a small cellarful of good wines. In its price range I will stack it against anybody's. My grandmother's departure from this life was the occasion of its founding, but I have kept it up ever since, as my purse permitted. There are ways, you know. For a priest, a good cassock costs about $100. It isn't really a vestment, only a kind of clerical smock, so that's a lot of money to spend on ecclesiastical overalls. Especially since the cheap outfits will sell you one for $18. Accordingly, my $100 worth of clothing money buys me one cotton-Dacron mail-order cassock and two cases of good claret. Every now and then of course someone tells me I look like a country parson. I just smile.

But the real dividend of my three generations of care is more subtle: I am sane on the subject of wine. Once in a while someone asks me if I drink. My answer is always: No; *drinking* is not a human activity. No man in his right mind can possibly set out "to drink" in the current sense of the phrase. Drinking, like Sex, is one of the big fake subjects. Of course I go on to explain to my questioner that I usually take a short vermouth at noon, a sherry or a *rince cochon* before dinner, a couple of glasses of Zinfandel, California Chablis, or better, with my meals, and not infrequently, a reasonable quantity of Scotch with my conversations. But I do not drink. My care is for the matter and the occasion, not for the activity of drinking. By a long love for the real subject, the fake one has been made to sit down and shut up.

As I said, however, I think the point is made. I care about music and I care about tools. And with fear and trembling, I ascend the ladder of care, not always caring enough, but at least generally aware of what care should look like. There is teaching and preaching; there is theology and Greek. My small cares are a good diagram; knowing what's involved in not blowing a minor subject is a real help in the great ones. Whether I have cared enough anywhere will be proved soon enough. Unless the Day of Judgment comes quickly, my children will testify for me or against me, and there will be no appeal from their witness. My fate is already in their hands.

IX

CHILDREN

The shortest and most incomplete guide to child-rearing presently available; the only treatment of the subject guaranteed not to make parents feel guilty.

BUT SEE WHAT HANDS THEY ARE that hold my fate. When I started out, I planned to give you a chapter about children, and to include in it a number of pieces of sage advice. Now that I have come to the point, however, I find that my fine generalities have dashed themselves to pieces against the six very concrete children that I have. I live surrounded by a mixture of violence and loveliness, of music and insensitivity. I take my meals with clods and poets, but I am seldom certain which is which. Nowhere is my life less reducible to logic than in my children; nowhere are my elegant attempts at system ground more violently to powder than under the stumbling stone of the next generation. Far from having advice to give you, I am dumbfounded by them, and I admit it. And yet I rejoice too, for nowhere is there so much to keep me sane. I apologize in advance, but I know only one word to describe it: It is *absurd*. I promise I shall not bring it up again, but it is the shank of the evening and with one more stick for the fire and one more drop in the bottle, there is nothing for it but to have one last go at saying it out: Absurdity is the touchstone of man's calling, and his children are the greatest of his teachers. Abraham learned it from Isaac, Joseph at the feet of the Child of Nazareth, and I under the hands of my own distracted mob; we are very different, we three, but the lessons are all the same. I am in good company; the school has distinguished alumni.

Unfortunately, the situation is complicated by my attendance at a competing school; I have other and contradictory teachers. In particular, I have a consulting psychologist in my head, who gives me a hard time. I cannot remember when, if ever, I retained this composite gentleman, or even in what scraps of popular psychology I met him. He is, to tell the truth, not much of a psychologist, but he is all I have around at the crucial moments. What he lacks in professional competence he more than makes up for by the ring of urgency and alarm he manages to get into his voice. He talks endlessly to me about Maturity and Adjustment, and about bringing my children to those blessed states with all deliberate speed. When things go well, he is pleasant enough; but when really dire things occur, when there appear in our local heavens the psychological signs of the end of the world—when beds are wet and thumbs are sucked, when achievement goes a-glimmering and hostilities are bared—he becomes tyrannical. He berates me with guilt, and torments me with failure. My response to all his lecturing is anything but adjustment; what he normally produces in me is panic and paralysis. If I could find a way to give him notice, I would fire him. Not because he's wrong, mind you (he's right—we are an ill-adjusted lot), but because he is mad. But since I cannot dismiss him, the next best thing is to ignore him. I will listen to my children instead. I will copy my answers from Abraham and Joseph. The old school is absurd, to be sure, but at least it is sane. Adjustment! To what can this riot of beings that is my household possibly be adjusted? The vision of finely tuned engines purring smoothly down the roads of their respective histories bears no resemblance to my waking hours. I shall consider myself lucky if, with coughing motor and slipping clutch, even one of them manages a clumsy career around the brink of disaster. Adjustment indeed! At their speed, and with their equipment, it can't be done.

Children are each generation's fresh witness to the bones of being under the fat of the word of man. In them, the skeleton of reality is still unfleshed and unadorned. They are a world and a chaos at once. Nobody sees logic more freshly and clearly than children, and no one uses it less. My work is indeed to form them in its ways, but

I cannot do it except absurdly. The word must be spoken to them, and the system imposed, and woe to the parent who shirks his calling. But equal woe if he thinks they will hear him. They are *surds*. They are *deaf*. Their parents, accordingly, are highly unprofitable servants.

But don't misunderstand. I do not love logic less because I love absurdity; I love it better. I do not revel in absurdity because it is irrational; I do it precisely because rationality without a sense of the absurd cannot stay rational even for five minutes. And through my children in particular, I begin to see that rationality is something more, and less, than I once thought. It is there, and there is no meaning and no life possible without it; but it is only the wind-rippled surface of the vast ocean of being. Beneath it are the depths from which we rose and into which we descend: Absurdity, Mystery.

The world will give a reasonable answer for everything except its own being; it makes marvelous sense, except that there is no sense in which it logically has to *be* at all. The shining spindrift of rationality blows across a sea of unnecessary existence. I look at my children. They chase each other with guns. There is a hill to be taken, a plan of attack and supply to be formed. Logistics and logic consume them. But do you know what I think; do you know what surprises me? Not that they play; certainly not that they play logically; and emphatically not that they play war. What surprises me is that they are here at all. Why should they be? Everything is unnecessary. The cancer in the blood and the blood it destroys;

the truck on the highway and the squirrel it crushes; and they and I and Joseph and Abraham, and earth and stars and sky and ocean. What are we doing here outside nothing? What do we mean, being *substantial?* The only possible answer is simply that God was pleased to make us so. But while the reply is intelligible in its form, it is absurd in its content: Our being, our substantiality, and our freedom are left with no reason other than his unsearchable counsel. The absurdity, you see, goes home to God. The mystery is not a mystery of appearance only; it lies buried in the heart of the Creator. At the end of all things Adam will not pass beyond absurdity; he will enter into it. As the flower of God's absurd will, as the least necessary of all his works, he will rise up to be confirmed forever in his unnecessary being. With risen body, risen mind, and risen will, with risen delight in Mozart and a risen love of pickles, the absurd will go home to the Absurd, and at the last reach of absurdity, find that he was never more comfortable in his life.

Behold, therefore, my children—the very diagram of unnecessary being. They are a world which matters but must not be taken seriously; in them I catch a glimpse of the ground line of incongruity, the root of laughter, the proof of God, the ladder of absurdity, the pearl of great price—the gem of logic mounted in the iron ring of existence and the whole piece set before my eyes to be assayed, bought and cherished by faith. Prophets and kings have died without seeing what I have seen. I am Joseph. To me, as to him, the absurd comes as a child, not for analysis but for holding, for trust, for faith. As a priest I sometimes say an old Latin prayer about St. Joseph; as a father I find its meaning driven home hard. *Non solum videre et audire*, not only to see and to hear, *sed portare, deosculari, vestire et custodire*, but to carry, to kiss, to clothe and to care for. *O felicem virum.* I am a happy man.

But if I am Joseph, I am also Abraham. Neither of them knew what they were doing. At the crucial moments, down at the roots of being, a man never knows *what*; only *whether* he was obeyed. Listen. *And Joseph being a just man was minded to put her away privily.* Joseph, sailing his fine course, beating skillfully to windward, with logic like spray breaking beautifully up over his bow, was minded to take the reasonable solution, to measure his risks and sail around them. *But God appeared to Joseph in a dream* and drowned him in the depths of absurdity; *and he took unto him Mary his wife, and knew her not...*The command to Joseph to accept the Seed of Abraham is no more comprehensible than the command to Abraham to destroy his seed; it is oracular and deaf to entreaty: *Take now thy son, thine only son Isaac, whom thou lovest, and get thee into the land of Moriah; and offer him there for a burnt offering upon one of the mountains which I will tell thee of.* And Abraham went, but he didn't know what he was doing. And neither did Joseph, and neither do I. And any man who says he does is either nodding or faking.

To assent to the birth of a child is not an exercise in logic, neither for Abraham, for Joseph nor for me; to live with them is to stretch rationality beyond its limits, for Abraham, for Joseph and for me. Abraham picked up the knife and fire the night that Isaac was conceived. I do the same. I have begotten them and I have reared them but I have no comments to make and no advice to give. I do not know if I have done them good or ill. I do not know whether, in their own generation, they will do well or badly; I cannot even guess whether they will build because of me or in spite of me. I know only that they will build elsewhere, and that I have here no continuing city. I can barely live with my children, yet I must shortly and inconceivably live without them. I have hardly known them, hardly begun to walk the streets of their minds and the gardens of their pleasures, hardly explored with them the city that they are, and already they begin to go their ways and to take my city with them. My exile comes implacably. By the waters of Babylon we sat down and wept when we remembered thee O Sion. If I forget thee O Jerusalem, let my right hand forget her cunning, let my tongue cleave to the roof of my mouth. I am absurd, I know; but it is the infirmity in which I glory. And therefore, though I have no advice, I shall speak nevertheless, only that I forget not Jerusalem, the shapes of her streets and the colors of her palaces. I shall stand upon my absurdity and bless my children.

MICHAEL, thou art my first-born, my might and the beginning of my strength, the excellency of dignity, and the excellency of power.

Michael goeth up first against the future; the rights of

the eldest are small recompense for his pains. His brethren shall stand in awe of him. He walks where none went before; he is a stranger where others will stand at ease.

My banner over him is urgency; he must not fail. He feedeth upon the bread of instruction, he drinketh discipline as the water of affliction; yet his heart sinketh not. Iron is in his hands and steel in his thoughts; he is abused, but he smiles and forgives.

His father is dumb and cannot speak. Michael is deaf and will not hear. Yet in the absurdity of their converse there is no misunderstanding; they allow each other's sticking points lightly; they end wars with winks.

His good nature shall refresh his household; he laugheth easily, he holdeth no grudge. Michael is a man without propriety; he will be a good friend. His mind shall be praised for balance and his will for coolness.

He is old for his years, but he weareth his age lightly; in a mad world his incongruity is a beacon of sanity.

> I met an old man who asked of me:
> How many strawberries grow in the sea?
> I answered him as I thought good:
> As many as red herrings grow in the wood.

He is nicely absurd. I rejoice that I met him on home ground.

ANNE is a lion's whelp. She is my life's November, warm and bleak by turns, and sweet and savage. She is my double and counter, my stone of stumbling and rock of offense. *It is not for kings, O Lemuel, it is not for kings to drink wine; nor for princes strong drink.*

O my soul, thou art come into deep waters. Anne is herself and no other; upon the hardness of her being, logic breaketh itself in pieces. Her brethren shall stop their mouths at her changing; but her constancy will be the lifting up of their heads. They shall labor in vain to reconcile her; yet shall she reconcile herself in her own season.

> Humpty Dumpty sat on a wall,
> Humpty Dumpty had a great fall;
> All the king's horses
> And all the king's men
> Cannot put Humpty Dumpty together again.

But Humpty Dumpty herself shall rise up and her enemies shall be sent empty away.

With a dictionary in his hand her brother came against her; he pointed triumphantly to the word she could not find. She returned him only her shoulder in acknowledgement, and her tongue in derision: "It wasn't there when *I* looked."

All the king's horses lie fallen in her wake; the king's men pant for breath.

STEPHEN is a strong ass, couching down between two burdens; and he saw that rest was good, and the land that it was pleasant.

The roof of his mouth is as the smell of apples; tastes

and sounds shall be his province, he shall yield royal dainties. His eyes shall be red with wine and his teeth white with milk. He discerneth goodness; greatness shall rest upon his table.

The blessings of thy father shall be upon the head of Stephen and on the crown of the head of him who was separate from his brethren: six months in a cast, one year in a hospital; out of his exile grew gentleness.

He hath long patience; but his short anger is fierce. He loveth justice, but by passion, and not easily; the archers shall sorely grieve him, and shoot at him. He sitteth down in peace, but if he rise up he shall shake himself in his indignation.

> Arthur O'Bower has broken his band
> He comes roaring up the land
> The King of Scots with all his power
> Cannot turn Arthur of the Bower.

Yet shall his force be but half his strength; his sweetness shall break bars of iron.

PATRICIA is a hind let loose: she giveth goodly words. Let her be blessed with the blessings of heaven above, blessings of the deep that lieth under, blessings of the breasts and of the womb.

Patricia shall be for an haven of ships; she is a world unto herself, a city that lacketh not. She maketh her dwelling in books, and her habitation in olden days.

The complaints of her brethren rise up against her;

she dreameth and her work falleth upon others. Yet will her idleness rebuke them; her dreams will work marvels where their deeds falter.

Blond, distracted, and distracting, she maketh princes to bow before her; loving, beloved, and for loving, her house shall be stronger than all kingdoms. *The heart of her husband shall safely trust in her, so that he shall have no need of spoil.*

> Hickamore Hackamore on the king's kitchen door
> All the king's horses
> And all the king's men
> Cannot drive Hickamore Hackamore off the king's kitchen door.

—Or draw my heart from your long hair, *svenska flicka.*

MARY, thou art she whom thy brethren shall praise; thy hand shall be in the neck of thine enemies, thy father's children shall bow down before thee.

Thou art beautiful, O my love, as Tirzah, comely as Jerusalem, terrible as an army with banners. Turn away thine eyes from me, for they have overcome me.

Mary flourisheth as the apple, but her heart is an heart of oak; her fragility troubleth the soul, yet the mind is astonished at the stability of her times.

Her household shall be peace and her habitation gentleness; the light of her countenance causeth war to cease.

She maketh herself coverings of tapestry, her clothing is silk and purple; they that sit at wine shall praise her.

Min skål
Din skål
Alla vackra flickors skål

We will remember thy love more than wine, O thou fairest, and thine incredible goodness more than strong drink.

VIRGINIA, a troop shall overcome her, but she shall overcome at the last; she groweth at the end of a fair garden; all those who pass by gaze upon her; she taketh astonishment as her due. *Many daughters have done virtuously, but thou excellest of them all.*

As a horse to the battle she rusheth among her sisters' goods. Destruction is in her hands, and desolation in the paths of her feet; she spoileth all their pleasant things.

Yet with soft looks she turneth away anger, and with her fingers she breaketh even hearts of steel.

> *Tummetott*
> *Slickepott*
> *Långeman*
> *Gullebrand*
> *Lilla vicke vire.*

No one, not even the rain, has such small hands.

X

THE MYSTICAL BODY

The theologian triumphant over the hobbyist (it was a fixed fight). The Author returns to his trade for a last attempt to pick up the loose stones of the City.

I HAVE STRUCK MYSELF DUMB. It is unsafe to look at the depth of one's involvement. I am utterly caught, yet I have so little to say to it all. If I am to do even a relatively honest job of finishing this book, I had better make promptly for the end before the choice between silence and talking through my hat becomes too painfully evident. With a minimum of parting comment, therefore, I shall begin to head for home.

Where am I? I have shown you my household: my private collection of outlandish people, fancy groceries and worn hardware. Am I very far from you? Is yours so

149

different? Are the results of your bed any less diverse or intractable than mine? Are the beings around your board any more intelligible? Do you know any more than I do what you are doing? Have you any better working knowledge of how to make a family? I don't think you do. And I don't think you think you do, either. I think we are all at sea. Not hopelessly lost, mind you, not even in terribly bad shape—just not doing very much brilliant navigation. Most of us are proceeding by guess and by gorry. We started out intelligibly enough, down plausible roads with confident steps. We married what we thought were likely people, and built households for what we thought were likely reasons, but it is all somewhat less than likely now. Husband, wife, children and things are only—are monumentally—themselves. The road of intelligibility has a way of running into the ditch of absurdity. Around sudden corners or blind turns, we have each of us been shunted off. I have moved upward and inward in my marriage, but in no way that I ever expected. I stand in awe of what I have done. Here we are, eight human beings, assembled in obedience to one bright proposal of mine. But whatever happened to my bright idea? It has long since gone dim in the blinding light of these individualities. Let me say it again: Life is not intelligible. The carefully planned steps that people take to fix it up are intelligible enough: Divorce is intelligible and contraception is intelligible and adjustment is intelligible and suicide is intelligible. But reality is not. The whole of being is precisely absurd. If this long monologue has any burden, it is that only the wholesale acceptance of the nonsense of actuality is sane; the little activities by which we jimmy reality into line with our notions are precisely mad. Here, however, I want to add something: It is that the acceptance of the absurdity of being is not so much an action in its own right as an entrance into another and larger action, which was going on long before we got around to doing anything. We do not actually achieve our goals; we achieve only the choice of our transportation; freedom is given to us, not to get us to our end, but to enable us to select the bus that will take us there. Staying in our seats is almost our noblest work.

I used to complain that I thought the Church's teaching on divorce had almost eclipsed the Church's teaching on marriage. What I meant was that if you asked most people what the Church's doctrine of marriage was, they would say simply: indissolubility. They would not be aware that she had anything to say about vocation, or about human nature as made in the image of God; only that she taught that once you got into it, you couldn't get out of it. I still think my complaint is just, but I'm not so sure any more that the situation is as serious as I once thought. It strikes me now that maybe indissolubility is the most important idea for the Church to get across after all. First, it has the advantage of being rather close to the words of Christ on the subject. Apart from one obscure remark about there being no marriage in heaven, the sum and substance of his recorded teaching on the subject was simply: no divorce. Second, it seems to be a little more germane to human nature as it really is than anything else I can think of. I have had lots of wonderful, if not fearful, ideas for my marriage, lots of intelligible plans and plausible projects for bringing it to the peak of perfection; but if you ask me now what I think was the best thing I ever did, I would say: staying with it. Not that there ever was, to tell the truth, much question of my leaving, but that in the modern world the idea, even as an impossibility, is never too far away. We spend a long time wishing we were elsewhere and otherwise. I have thought, as who has not, of other wives and different children, of better circumstances and more likely companions. I have made my share of comparisons. But staying with the bus remains the most brilliant thing I have done. As the years pass, the comparisons begin to be visibly irrelevant, and the actualities blossom in their own strange way. Ever so slowly, the words "I wish I hadn't" or "If only I had" fade from the vocabulary, and the odd shape of the bus itself begins to fill and delight the mind. A long time ago, the children of Israel had some highly intelligible for- eign treaties in prospect. They wanted to take their logical place among the nations of the world. God, however, sent them the prophet Isaiah, who advised them to forget the whole business and mind the knitting they actually had. Your strength is to sit still, was the way he put it; and it applies very nicely now to all the plausible little Egyptian alliances that still surround us. Your strength is to sit still. Don't get off the bus.

But just what is the bus? The time has come to stop

being foxy and allusive and to try to say it out. Basically it is what I've been referring to all along as the City or the Mystical Body. It's the fundamental fact that the created order manifests a built-in tendency by which all things seek to become one through membership in each other. This tendency is, as I have said, the creaturely counterpart of the coinherence of the three Persons of the Godhead— Father, Son and Holy Ghost—and there isn't a thing in the world that doesn't show it forth somehow. The social aspects of life are the clearest diagrams of it, but it's marriage that is the most elegant diagram of all. Entrance into marriage is precisely entrance into an already designed pattern of coinherence. There is, of course, a good deal in marriage that needs doing and thinking about, but even granting all that, it's the shape of the matrimonial bus itself that is still the biggest single factor—the one that will make me or break me. My actions must be suitable to the thrust of coinherence that is already built into the nature of marriage; otherwise I am asking for frustration and disaster. It's like the physical growth of children. I take care of feeding them, but it's the native tendencies of their bodies that take care of the growth. I am not the author of their stature, only the cultivator of it. And it's the same in marriage. I am not in any straight-line sense the builder of my marriage. Marriage, as an institution, was built when Adam was, and in my own particular case, it would be reasonable to assume that the shapes of many possible marriages were waiting for me long before I even thought of the subject. My work now, since I have chosen one of them, is not so much to create it in the image of some abstract ideal perfection, but to cooperate with it as it labors to disclose its true coinherent shape to me. I am not the agent of my matrimonial destiny; I am only its midwife.

At this point, however, I want to avoid a misunderstanding. I am talking about a real bus, not a mental one. When I use the word coinherence, I do not take it to be simply an interpretive principle. I am using it to refer to a very specific fact, namely, that the Creator himself is coinherent, and that he has made the created order to be a reflection of his coinherence. I mean by it what orthodox Christians have always meant by it: that the three Persons of the Godhead mutually indwell each other in act and essence, and that the world which they have made has analogous tendencies. Let me try to state it in fairly plain theological language.

Christians believe that God is one, but that in the oneness of the Godhead there are, by a high mystery, three coequal Persons: the Father, the Son and the Holy Ghost. As if that weren't paradoxical enough, they go on to add that the three Persons are in no sense three parts of God, but that each possesses in himself the fullness of the Godhead. To make the riddle even harder, they also insist that while the three Persons are distinct, they nevertheless exist and act together in the one divine substance of Godhead, *and that they therefore mutually indwell each other*, so that the Father is in the Son, and the Holy Ghost in the Father, and so on, but without confusion. This is the

154

aspect of the doctrine that goes by the name of coinherence, or to use the Latinism, circumcession. But then, by a kind of *O Altitudo* of absurdity, they add that in this marvel of coinherent and coequal three-in-oneness, there is a deeper mystery still: The Father alone is the fountainhead of divinity. Not, of course, by way of physical origin or temporal priority (for they are all simply *one God*), but by a marvel of initiation and obedient response which is referred to as the Divine Monarchy of the Father. The Son and the Holy Ghost —fully God though each of them is, coinherent in each other and in the Father though both of them are—the Son and the Holy Ghost do nothing of themselves. Their whole divine will is simply to do the will of the Father. *I came not to do mine own will, but the will of him that sent me*, says Jesus of himself, *I do always the things that please him. He shall not speak of himself*, says Jesus of the Holy Ghost, *but whatsoever he shall hear, that shall he speak.*

The picture therefore begins to emerge. The world is the way it is, because God is the way he is. The act of Creation is a divine lark by which the Persons of the Trinity chose to embody, in a discrete and granular world, an analogical reflection of their own mutuality. The created order of pieces and parts becomes the image of the coinherence. It is the mutuality of the world that is its greatest wonder. Nothing is outside it. From obvious instances like the kitten nursing at its mother's side or the cohesiveness of the structure of the atom, to the less obvious ones like the mutuality by which the rabbit eats the lettuce and the lion eats the rabbit and the crow picks the carcass of the lion, the whole order is coinherent. It isn't all roses, but on its own level it makes a very Godlike garden.

And the picture becomes even clearer when you look at the parts of the world that are capable of more than instinctive response—when you look at men, with their reason and their freedom. They are the ones who reflect the *O Altitudo* itself. The grandest of the world's coinherences are precisely the human ones: the civic and corporate entities which men have always so abundantly brought forth. Every human society, from the family to the state, from the Barnum Avenue Blue Ribbon Girls' Club to the United Nations, strains to become the mystical body; every time there is the least chance of hierarchy it forms: The college of cardinals and the possessors of keys to the executive washroom are up to the same thing. The mutualities of cat and kitten, of crow and carcass, are not enough for us. We cannot stop at coinherence; even at our most democratic we press on to imitate the divine monarchy.

In one of the most refined statements of the doctrine of the Trinity, the three Persons are referred to as *subsistent relations* within the Godhead. Pass the word *subsistent*; it's important, but not here. The key word is relations. It is in the relational aspects of man's nature that the image of God can be most clearly seen. This is true first of all on the relatively low level of the relation of the various parts of his nature to each other: Heart and liver, reason and will are members one of another, and serve their turns in a hierarchical dance. But it is true all the way across the board. Men are related to each other in mutuality and hierarchy. There is no choice about *whether* they will be, only *how*. We have control only of the modalities of membership; the fact of the city is not a matter of choice. Divine or demonic, the city itself will never fail to appear; natural or perverse, the body of the mystery will always come to birth. Heaven is the flowering of the coinherence and hell is a monstrous parody of it, but they are both cities; the annihilation of six million Jews contributed to the demonic mutuality and the satanic hierarchy of Nazi Germany. In friendship and in family, in the club, the village, the nation and the Church, mankind is engaged in an essay in membership, in an attempt to achieve the heavenly Jerusalem. We may do well or badly, but we can do no other. We are made in the image of the coinherent God.

One clarification. In talking about the tendency of the world toward membership, I have waxed flowery. I should say plainly that it is only a fact; it is not a mystique. It is in no sense a key or a gimmick by which the Real Recipe for Life can be derived. It is just one more aspect of reality which, like all the other aspects, can be perfected or perverted. This is a necessary warning, because it's all too easy to get the idea that the world is possessed of a kind of *élan vital* which is going to run its own sacred course willy-nilly. I don't mean that. All I mean is that the world has a shape, and that its shape is membership—the city. I have not said that the particular cities that actually do form are necessarily either inevitable or good. No fatalism, no eudaemonism, only fact. To be sure, Christians believe that the world will, in the end, turn out to have a very definite order indeed—that it will become nothing less than the City of God: The kingdoms of this world will become the kingdom of our God and of his Christ. But the crucial thing to notice here is that they will not get that way by a straight-line progress. By nature, the world is only *apt* to be the Body; it takes grace to make it so in fact. Death and resurrection, cataclysm and judgment come between us and our continuing City. The heavenly Jerusalem is precisely heavenly.

The warning is necessary, because whatever we may say about the way the world might have developed without sin, the fact of sin throws a rather large monkey wrench into the works of coinherence. Adam without the fall might well have drawn the created order into membership in a fairly straight line, but that's only speculation now. The fallen world is still the image of the coinherence, but even its natural aptness to become the City doesn't count too heavily against the divisiveness of sin. As a matter of fact, the city takes a rather bad beating among us, and most of the actual instances of it have a generous trace of the demonic in them. And it was ever thus, at least since the day that Adam walked glumly out of the Garden of Eden to look for a home.

It is the wandering destiny of Adam in search of the City that is the real subject matter of the Bible. Genesis begins with the othering of the coinherence, by the creation of matter and of man in the image of God; and Revelation ends with the flowering of that image in the descent of the New Jerusalem as a bride adorned for her husband. But for 1,186 chapters in between, it is a series of detours: the achievement of the City, not by the working out of a natural mystique, but by cataclysms, absurdities and indirections. There is a line, and it goes with unerring step to its appointed end, but it is anything but straight. Adam is made in the first chapter of Genesis, established in the second, and fallen by the end of the third. The City, so briefly glimpsed, has vanished in a snowstorm of buck-passing; the coinherence of matter has disappeared in a thicket of thorns, thistles and death. The rest of Scripture is the story of its complex restoration. The heart of the matter is of course the Incarnation of the Coinherent Word Himself in Jesus, but that is the end of the story. Near the beginning of the Bible, there are two chapters which will serve very well as an epitome of the whole process.

In the eleventh chapter of the Book of Genesis there occurs the story of the Tower of Babel; in the twelfth there is the account of the call of Abraham. There they sit, back to back, the perfect diagram of the city as it really is in a fallen world. Babel is the flower of the kind of intelligibility that has reigned since the day that the serpent started chopping logic with Eve. It is the granddaddy of all the shipwrecks of the straight-line approach. *Go to, let us build us a city and a tower, whose top may reach unto heaven; and let us make us a name, lest we be scattered abroad upon the face of the whole earth.* Abraham, on the other hand, is the monument of absurdity. *Get thee out of thy country, and from thy kindred, and from thy father's house, unto a land that I will shew thee.* Babel is a city of builders, but they do not build the City. It is a wanderer who becomes the father of the People of the coinherence. Babel is logical as the serpent was logical; it is man trying to do something intelligible *to* the world. Abraham is absurd as the gift of being itself is absurd; he is man trying to do something obedient *with* the world. Babel is the disaster of the plausible; Abraham is the triumph of the odd.

For Babel finally frustrated its own efforts. The Tower was precisely a violation of the coinherence. It was a love, not of reality but of what reality could be made to mean. It was a reversal of the true role of man. Out of the ground of the Garden of Eden *the Lord God formed every beast of the field, and every fowl of the air; and brought them unto Adam to see what he would call them: and whatsoever Adam called every living creature, that was the name thereof.* Intellect faced the world in love. Adam, the priest of creation, looked upon the real being of each thing, called its name, and lifted it into the measures of the dance. At Babel, a fallen Adam looks not at real being, but at the meaning which his mind chooses to force upon it. In consequence, he proceeds straight to the construction of the world's first architectural monstrosity—the first recorded instance of something built by people who cared more for their ideas than for their materials. *And they had brick for stone, and slime had they for mortar.* They would have used sheep manure if it could have been made to stand up. All they cared about was the result, but that they never got. The mercy of God came down and cut off their loveless labor before it overran the world. There are some things that should not be shared: In Eden, speech was born; at Babel, God reduced Adam to gibberish lest he speak the word which would build the city of hell. *So the Lord scattered them abroad from thence upon the face of all the earth; and they left off to build the city.*

They left off. But God didn't. All the ancient penalties are the work of Mercy Himself. Man is punished by death, only to be saved by death. And at Babel, man is deprived of intelligibility only that his sanity may be restored by absurdity. The eleventh chapter of Genesis declares the bankruptcy of fallen reasonableness; in the twelfth, the city goes into an absurd receivership, to be built, not in the land of Shinar, nor in any homely or likely place, but on the roads and deserts of the ancient world. Not with bricks but by obedience, not with knowledge, but by faith, Abraham the wanderer lays the first course of stones and the great work sets forward. The mystery of the coinherence begins again to prevail; the city that lieth foursquare begins to appear. Its builders are strangers and pilgrims. From the children of Israel to the Catholic Church, we have here no continuing city, but the mystery of the city works in us. The mercy has come full circle; the loss itself becomes the means of restoration. It is the homeless who know the most about home; it is the wanderers among whom the city is formed.

But enough. The excursion has gone sufficiently far to prove that the bus has some remarkable connections. My marriage is precisely the absurd Abrahamic call to build the City by obedience. It is to be entered not in the hope that I am choosing the peculiarly, intelligibly, right transportation to the goal of my heart's desire, but with a determination to ride whatever bus I happen to get on to the end of the line. And faith is the only root that can produce the determination. Only faith got Abraham to Moriah, and only faith will keep me faithful. But the great thing is that it really will—if only I keep the Faith. For the City is not a distant goal; it is already within me. My baptism into the body of Christ, my membership in the mystery of the coinherence, is no mere idea. I have been joined substantially to the risen humanity of Jesus which is the center of the City of God. By real union with that Holy Thing, born of Mary, and crucified, risen and ascended, I enter the exchanges of the Mystical Body. And my marriage enters with me.

Of course it is all absurd. I try to imagine what orthodox Christianity must seem like to outsiders. I cannot see how it can sound anything but appalling. It is purely and simply outlandish. But there you have the last secret, the mystery hidden in God from the foundation of the world. In a creation that has violated the coinherence, the true City will always seem *outlandish*, and its members will always look like foreigners. The City of God grows only in the desert, and strangers and pilgrims are its builders. All of its true exchanges will, to the extent that they are true, be absurd. From music to marriage, from drawing to death, every real act of the coinherence will always be unintelligible to the children of this world. They are wiser in their generation than the children of light.

Nevertheless, therefore—and therefore nevertheless—I rejoice. My strength is to sit still, and I am content to do it. My bed and board are the choice places of my healing and I go to them with a glad mind. God wills to build the City, but while he makes it *matter*, he refuses to make it *serious*. The divine mirth lies behind all things and it is in his light that I begin to see the lightness of it all.

The same stone which the builders refused is become the headstone in the corner. This is the Lord's doing, and it is marvelous in our eyes. God is the Lord who hath showed us light; bind the sacrifice with cords, yea, even unto the horns of the altar.

DINNER AT OUR HOUSE

The City unveiled at last. A vision of Jerusalem as it now appears: not descending in glory from above, but rising in embarrassed majesty from a sea of arguments, spilled milk and uneaten broccoli.

FATHER: Bless ye.

ANSWER: *Bless ye.*

FATHER: The eyes of all wait upon thee, O Lord;

ANSWER: *And thou givest them their meat in due season.*

FATHER: Thou openest thine hand;

ANSWER: *And fillest all things living with plenteousness.*

FATHER: Glory be to the Father, and to the Son, and

to the Holy Ghost;

ANSWER: *As it was in the beginning, is now, and ever shall be, world without end. Amen.*

FATHER: Let us pray.
Bless, O Lord, these gifts to our use, and us to thy service, through Christ our Lord.

ANSWER: *Amen.*

A CHILD: Bid, Sir, a blessing.

FATHER: May the King of Eternal Glory make us partakers of his heavenly table.

ANSWER: *Amen.*

I look down the table over which I preside. I feel like God partway through Creation. Before me stretches a chaos only half turned into a world. By paternal fiat, by the words of the grace before meat, the half-hinted shape of a cosmos gathers, hangs for a moment in trembling order, and promptly collapses into discreteness and solitariness again. Self, wife, sons, daughters; dishes, silver, food. Where is the City in all this? Why is it so long in forming among us?

My carving tools rest now upon an intractable leg of lamb (presented wrong side up—my wife cooks marvelously; why doesn't she look at what she does?). No matter: *Pax tranquillitas ordinis*; let the orderer speak the next fiat. Unfortunately, others are already talking. Creation is hurling back a flood of *caveats* and *non placets* at its creator. My first-born must have no gravy on his rice;

166

the third-begotten begs off the mushrooms. My eldest daughter loves lamb of course, but not that much. In imitation of the divine largesse, I ply the serving spoons. I am diffusive of rice and broccoli, and of straying peas that roll off into the void like superfluous planets. But my creation returns me uncivil answers: "This piece is all fat." "I can't eat that many carrots."

"Quiet! You are all on silence!" It is a pretty negative fiat, but it works, and in the shuffling stillness the hint of order comes again. I quote them St. Paul on the subject of pots talking back to the potter. I remind them they are a city, not a mob, and in return for having taken them in off the streets of non-being, I expect some manners and mutuality. The older ones agree. My heart lifts: The City is at least somewhat built. And the youngest knocks over a glass of milk. Down toward me it races like a flood across the land. I jump up and back, but over the edge it pours and I am hit; right trouser leg, below the knee. It is the third time this meal and the sixth or ninth or thousandth today. My largesse is as nothing next to the cataract of milk she has produced in three short years. And my inventiveness small—she has spilled it backhand, forehand, sidearm and elbow first. She has upset glasses with her head, her feet, her shoulders and knees; with her rump, her belly and the middle of her back. And with endless variety of time and circumstance. Upon thick tablecloths yielding a white swamp which spreads ominously toward us all; or upon plastic tablecloths for a high-velocity attack. (I can remember only one successful escape from milk spilled on plastic. I nearly broke the chair to do it.) And she has spilled it before, during and after meals, by commission and omission, and with enough broken glass to rival the divine scattering of the hoarfrost.

The ban on talk is lifted. Person confronts person again and the dance of human converse slowly begins. The two eldest are going to the city with their grandmother, and the subject of department stores and the Christmas rush invites us. Someone recalls the image of the ground floor of Macy's Herald Square store seen from the top of the escalator: We become the City analyzing the city. It goes well, prescinds from the general and moves on to more specialized stores: F.A.O. Schwarz is lifted up with its $300 ship models and $500 doll houses. I tell my story about Uncle Hobart buying soap in Henri Bendel's. But my second daughter is silent. The corner of my eye catches her, head lowered. I know what it is. "Patricia! Get rid of that book!" She is on her twenty-ninth Nancy Drew mystery and has smuggled it to the table to read in her lap. I command her to mind present realities, to mingle in the meeting of minds. She looks up, and I turn back to the others. But the meeting has adjourned. Two are arguing and three are talking at once: The City has collapsed again and the desert and the jungle return. "Finish *everything* on your plates!"

Conversation has come and gone, leaving no trace. Perhaps, in view of the tender age of my creatures, I have expected too much of them. The fiat of personal encounter having failed, I resort to the simpler fiat of common work. I give the order to clear for dessert. What ensues however is not activity, but a discussion ranging over the past six or eight weeks, on the subject of just who had the job of stacking the dishwasher when; (no one wants to clean the counters). Four budding Philadelphia lawyers meet head on. Questions of evidence, principles of equity, claims of indemnification and complaints of discrimination rise up before me. I gavel them to order with the flat of my hand: "Settle your own hash or I'll settle it for you." The silver jumps, a wineglass falls and the case is thrown out of court. They rise and head for the kitchen. The fiat of work has been uttered.

But no work has been done. No dish has moved, no crumb been brushed, no chutney-covered spoon lifted from the chaos before me. My spirit broods upon the face of spilled milk and upset wine; over a deep strewn with rinds and crusts and soggy paper napkins, without form and void. "Get back in here, all of you!" They return through the dining room door, without words. Three feet from me one of them doubles up, lurches to the wall and screams in tears, "Michael hit me!" In all my years with them, I have never actually seen it happen—how they manage the surreptitious right to ribs, or the invisible elbow in the solar plexus. All I see is normality followed by inexplicable mayhem; the sounds of the city swallowed up in the wail of the savage wounded by a phantom.

But they do clear finally. And the chocolate soufflé with whipped cream (my wife *is* a marvelous cook) draws us together in praise. There are prayers and we sing: four shaky parts with a counter-melody of free advice, carping criticism, and uncontrollable pre-schoolers. It is not the heavenly Jerusalem, but neither is it chaos. We are the solitary set in family. I love them all, their faces and voices, their bodies, their minds; and I thank them for their company these long short years.

ABOUT THE AUTHOR

Robert Farrar Capon was an Episcopal priest, writer, and chef who authored many books during his lifetime, all of which insisted on good humor, good food, and the mercy of God. He lived with his wife, Valerie, on Shelter Island in NY, until he passed away in 2013.

ACKNOWLEDGEMENTS

For the publication of this book, we are indebted first and foremost to Robert's wife, Valerie Capon, who so generously chose us to help resurrect his work and who has provided invaluable and insightful guidance throughout the process. Thank you to the Rt. Rev. C. Andrew Doyle and the Episcopal Diocese of Texas, and to the Rt. Rev. Scott Benhase and the Episcopal Diocese of Georgia, for their support of Mockingbird and especially of this project; to the Rev. Mark Strobel, Tom Martin, David Peterson, Margaret Pope, Jeff Dillenbeck, and CJ Green; to all of our readers, donors, and supporters—thank you.

ABOUT MOCKINGBIRD

Founded in 2007, Mockingbird is an organization devoted to connecting the Christian faith with the realities of everyday life in fresh and down-to-earth ways. We do this primarily, but not exclusively, through our publications, conferences, and online resources. To find out more, visit us at mbird.com or e-mail us at info@mbird.com.

ALSO FROM MOCKINGBIRD

The Mockingbird Quarterly

The Mockingbird Devotional
Good News for Today (and Everyday)

Law and Gospel: A Theology for Sinners (and Saints)
by Will McDavid, Ethan Richardson, and David Zahl

Unmapped: A Spiritual Memoir Duet
by Charlotte Getz & Stephanie Phillips

Churchy: The Real Life Adventures of a Wife, Mom, and Priest
by Sarah Condon

Mockingbird at the Movies

A Mess of Help
From the Crucified Soul of Rock N'Roll
by David Zahl

Eden and Afterward: A Mockingbird Guide to Genesis
by Will McDavid

PZ's Panopticon
An Off-the-Wall Guide to World Religion
by Paul F.M. Zahl

Grace in Addiction
The Good News of Alcoholics Anonymous for Everybody
by John Z.

This American Gospel
Public Radio Parables and the Grace of God
by Ethan Richardson

*Our books are available at mbird.com/publications or on Amazon, and our
quarterly magazine can be found at magazine.mbird.com.*

Made in the USA
Middletown, DE
06 September 2021